Americana

Roadside Memories

Americana

Roadside Memories

GAS FOR LESS
NATIONAL CREDIT CARDS HONORED

Arrows

Leather Bags

Michael Karl Witzel and Tim Steil
Additional photography by Jim Luning

Lowe & B. Hould
Publishers

On the front cover, left: The Route 66 Visitor Center in Hackberry, Arizona. *Jim Luning*. **Top right:** Roadside diners, cafes, and drive-ins offered classic American fare such as hamburgers and fries, with popular tunes available at the touch of a button. *© 2003 Michael Karl Witzel/Coolstock.com*. **Bottom right:** This postcard from the 1940s depicts Tijeras Canyon in New Mexico, one of the many interesting twists and turns along America's Route 66. *© 2003 Coolstock.com Collection*

On the back cover: A collage of Route 66 images recalls the days of cheap gas, personal service, and carefree travel. *© 2003 Michael Karl Witzel/Coolstock.com*

On the title page: Roadside stops along Route 66 like the Big Arrows Trading Post in Houck, Arizona, offered fuel for the car and for the stomach. *© 2003 Coolstock.com Collection.*

ISBN 0-681-62683-6

Printed in China

Contents

Route 66

Gas Station Memories

Drive-In Deluxe

Route 66

I suppose there are people in this world who are unaffected by the smell of diesel smoke. That, leaning against a truck stop gas pump at 3 AM, a warm summer breeze full of corn pollen, and exhaust fumes bathing them would not give them an urge to purchase a tall coffee, jump on the nearest highway and drive until daylight just to see what's there. I am suspicious of them.

There are few things in life as alluring as a road trip, and few roads beckon as seductively as Route 66. Stretching halfway across the country to the Pacific, it is a road born of necessity and sustained by sheer will. There are more scenic trips, perhaps, but none more encompassing of the twentieth-century American experience than Route 66.

There has been much written about this road over the years. There are many wonderful books, maps, and videos out there that go into far greater detail than I have room for. But many only talk about Route 66 in the past tense, as if it ceased to exist simply because fewer people travel it today. Or worse yet, they tend to look at everything along the road through teary eyes, lamenting the sorry state of things since the interstates went in. That's unfair.

Yes, there are whole sections of the road that are gone, where the pavement simply stops and turns into a muddy field. There are restaurants and motels and gas stations and entire towns that dried up and blew away when the interstate bypassed them. I've peered through their dusty windows, picked through their old business records, and been chased down their abandoned main streets by dogs who,

Preface

apparently with nothing better to do, take great solace in watching overgrown men run and swear at the same time.

So while you'll find a bit of familiar history inside, there are also things I've left out—stories others have already told better. I tried to find some new faces and places along the way, and perhaps take a more thoughtful look at the ones we all know. It's easy to get caught up in the nostalgia and kitsch of what Route 66 was 50 years ago, but I am just as interested, if not more so, in what it is today.

I did a lot of research before leaving on this trip. I read all the books, watched all the documentaries, and studied the maps. Though I left with a good historical grounding, it did little to actually prepare me for the enormity of the experience. I've traveled extensively in my life—all over the world—but driving Route 66 from end to end has been the absolute journey of a lifetime.

I met beautiful, kind people who would give you their last dollars and the shirts off their backs if they thought you truly needed it, and toothless, drunken rednecks who would gladly cut your throat from ear to ear simply because you're not "from here." But mostly I met average folks, respectful of one another and carrying on from day to day as best they can.

This old road is a subtle teacher, and the lessons I learned along the way will be with me forever. Anyway, glad you decided to come along. Don't mess with the radio.

—*Tim Steil*

During infrequent trips back to Arizona, famed artist Bob Waldmire is working on "the world's largest map of Old Route 66" outside of Meteor City.

Downtown Chicago is an eerie place at sunrise. There is a brief window where the shifts of the night owls and overachievers don't quite meet, and the Loop is almost still. It's 6:30 in the morning, and between the long shadows there are already crowds of people scurrying along the sidewalks and across the streets. On Michigan Avenue you can hear a faint hum of traffic from Lake Shore Drive under the cabs' horns and cops' whistles. In two hours there will be hundreds of thousands of people jamming into offices and onto roadways and sidewalks.

Rolling west out of the Loop and onto Ogden Avenue you get a glimpse of a different side of Chicago. The shiny steel and glass canyon gives way to vacant lots and corner bodegas where more business gets done out on the sidewalk than in the store. Storefront churches and liquor stores sit in uneasy proximity as Route 66 slices through the city's southwest side. There are few reminders of the old road here—certainly no souvenir stands. While we tend to think of places affected by the closing of Route 66 as being rural, its decommissioning was as devastating to the inner city as it was to small-town

You can't get there from here. Though Michigan and Jackson is technically the beginning of Route 66, Jackson runs one way east. To leave downtown Chicago you must jog one block south and turn west on Adams.

CHAPTER 1

Illinois

Shiny Side Up, Muddy Side Down

America. If here, along the Chicago-Cicero border they seem to miss it less, it is because they have lost so much of everything.

But by the time you get to Harlem Avenue things perk back up. The brown-and-white historical markers reappear, guiding you through the last of the exurban sprawl of Chicago and onto Interstate 55 for a stretch. Here the southbound lanes are old Route 66, and just off one of the first exits is Dell Rhea's Chicken Basket.

Dell Rhea's Chicken Basket

As you walk in, Pat Rhea is seated at the bar, one eye on the television, the other alternating between a waitress and the *Wall Street Journal*. He listens intently to the phone cocked to his left ear while he waves to someone walking in the door. The garrulous owner of Dell Rhea's Chicken Basket is a busy man. He is also a lucky man.

The restaurant his father took over in the early 1960s is an oddball along old 66—a survivor. It sits a few hundred feet from Interstate 55 in Willowbrook, Illinois, dually insulted by a frontage road address and maze of chain hotels surrounding it.

The chicken comes in a light batter, and the live music comes hot and greasy. When we visited, Pat Smillie, a Scotsman with a voice like Delbert McClinton and a build like a keg of beer, was belting out Parliament/Funkadelic covers and dancing off his 102-degree fever.

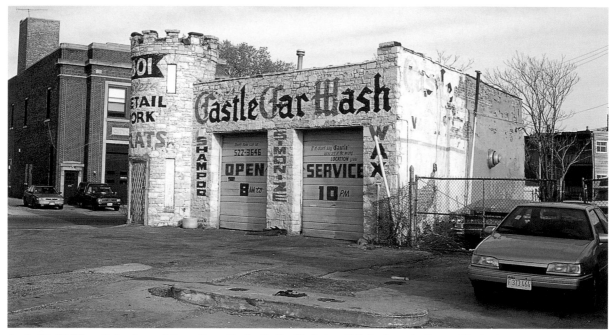

Route 66, US 34, or Ogden Avenue? Regardless, the Castle Car Wash does little business in Cicero, Illinois. Once home to mobsters such as Al Capone and Frank Maltese, the suburb has never been able to live down its "wide-open" reputation.

The Chicken Basket is as old as Route 66 itself. In 1927 Irv Kolarik ran a gas station across the street. Inside he had a little counter and a few booths, and soon realized he liked cooking better than getting his hands dirty at the gas station. Four sisters from a nearby farm offered to teach him how to fry chicken and work for him, if he would buy his chicken and eggs from their farm.

The sisters eventually married and left Kolarik the recipe and the business. He closed his repair bays and turned them into additional dining rooms, but a dispute with his landlord forced him out of the building. He sold the business to the landlord, and immediately bought the property across the street. A year to the day later, when a noncompete clause had expired, Kolarik opened the "Nationally Famous Chicken Basket" in its current location. That night Dell Rhea, who ran the Woodbine Restaurant up the street, closed up and personally led all his customers over.

"It was his way of paying tribute to the new owner, and saying welcome to the neighborhood," says Pat. In an odd twist of fate, his father would end up buying the restaurant from Kolarik less than 20 years later.

Dell Rhea was well known and respected in the area and added his name to the business. His combination of charisma and connections soon turned the place around. A supper club in its finest classic sense, it became a favorite for locals and travelers.

While he has managers who handle the day-to-day transactions, Rhea is constantly tweaking the menu, monitoring his advertising and marketing plan, and eating chicken. The staff knows at any time he may walk in and check an order. In short time, you realize two things: Pat Rhea cares deeply about what he does, and a lot more thought goes into a fried chicken dinner than you ever considered.

Every place that serves fried chicken touts a secret recipe, and Rhea assures us he has one too. Though

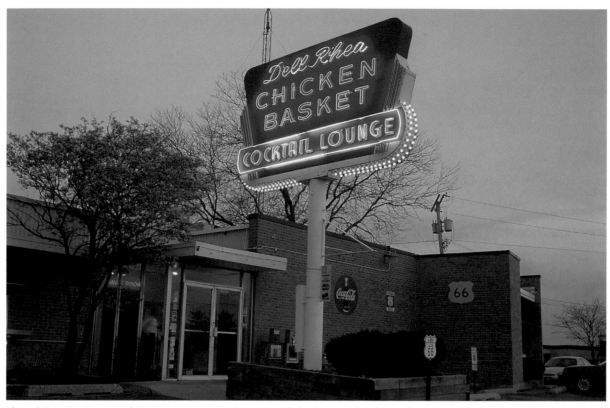

If you follow the signs carefully, you can navigate the maze of frontage roads it takes to find Dell Rhea's Chicken Basket. Inside Pat and Grace Rhea serve up hot food, good music, and Route 66 "Route Beer," bottled by a friend.

he won't be specific about ingredients he says there are some differences between his chicken and others.

"We season the meat. Most places only put seasonings in the batter. And we never use frozen chickens," he explains. "The size is very important as well. Too small a bird dries out when you cook it, and the bigger chickens tend to be fatty. We only use ones within a certain weight range."

Yet for all his passion and expertise, Rhea never intended to go into the family business. "I saw the way my parents had to work, and the sacrifices we had to make. We missed weddings, funerals, and all sorts of family obligations."

Though he had been accepted into an accelerated prelaw program at DePaul University, Pat attended a local community college so he could continue to work at the restaurant while he attended classes. And though he took classes in business law and management, he also enrolled in food service courses.

The Chicken Basket's reputation today is international. As Rhea describes a customer from the night before, who had the place recommended to him while waiting for a flight in London's Heathrow Airport, a waitress brings over a book in Japanese on Route 66 that a visiting couple wants autographed. He excuses himself to go talk to the couple, whose command of English is limited mostly to nodding and smiling.

"Stuff like that just gives me the chills," he says, taking a long pull on his drink as he sits back down a few minutes later. "Just gives me the chills."

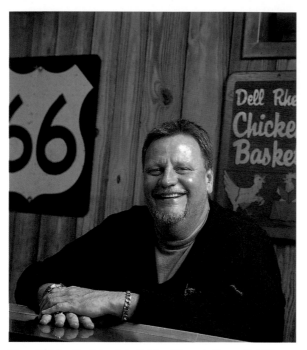

"I won't drive the interstate if I don't have to," says Pat Rhea. He got as far as Shamrock, Texas, on Route 66, where he and a friend schemed to buy the U-Drop Inn. Today Rhea is eyeing neighboring suburbs to open new locations and hopes someday to take the restaurant national.

Circa 1950. Irv Kolarik's "Nationally Famous" chicken recipe actually came from four sisters on a nearby goat farm, who worked as cooks and waitresses. Despite being bypassed by Interstate 55, the Chicken Basket has been open in this location for over 50 years. *Dell Rhea's Chicken Basket*

Illinois Icons

Rolling into the widening prairie south of Dwight, the old road runs parallel to the older road, which, were it not for the grass growing through the cracks in it, seems to be in drivable shape. Just outside Towanda, Club 66 sits in humble defiance. Once a service station, the pumps and islands have been painted over in funky, park-bench green and the oil company sign replaced with a crudely rendered 66 logo. Inside, locals enjoy an early beer and the latest news from their neighbors, though no one is sure who owns the bright red Corvette parked on old 66 across the way. Yet another riddle on a lost highway.

The miles south of Bloomington are rich in Route 66 lore. Here, the Funk family has been tapping sugar maples since the 1800s. Their "sirup" (spelled that way to indicate it is made without added sugar) has long been a staple of travelers. And for those whose schedules don't permit a drive on the actual road, the Dixie Truckers Home offers a one-stop look at the history of Route 66.

J. P. Walters opened the original Dixie Truckers Home in a converted garage in 1928. It soon developed a reputation among long-haul truckers for its good food and southern hospitality. Even throughout the Depression, as many businessmen fell on hard times, Walters' cafe flourished. Soon, travelers were coming around the clock, and Walters decided to stay open 24 hours a day. The world's first truck stop was born.

In the 70-some years since, the Dixie Truckers Home has only closed once, when it was destroyed by fire in 1965. Still, as the remains of the building smoldered nearby, the pumps reopened for business.

Next Page
So much for little green men. The Gemini Giant towers over Route 66 at the Launching Pad Drive-In in Wilmington. Next door, cars wait in line at the Route 66 Car Wash.

Businesses change along Route 66. What was once a modern gas station is now home to Club 66, a makeshift tavern.

The Dixie Truckers Home you encounter today is bright, clean, and sparkling new. Inside, an old-fashioned buffet is flanked by a retro soda fountain. There is a modern convenience store and gift shop, plus showers, arcades, and phones, amenities you probably don't realize the importance of unless you are a long-haul trucker. And tucked in back between the restrooms and the video arcade is the Route 66 Museum.

It's no more than a hallway, really, but in the 30 or so feet of glass-cased displays are some true gems. A Route 66 highway sign that was used in the filming of the television series of the same name sits beside sheet music of the Nat King Cole hit, "(Get Your Kicks on) Route 66," and a bowling league patch from a team sponsored by the Chicken Basket Restaurant, before it became Dell Rhea's Chicken Basket. And off to one corner is a large photo of a man in a tall chef's hat, sitting on a chair in the middle of a crumbling blacktop road. The road is Route 66; the man in the hat is Ernie Edwards.

For 54 years Edwards ran the Pig Hip Restaurant in Broadwell. Though it closed in 1991, he still lives next door, and is eager to talk about Route 66 with those who pass. When we rolled up late one afternoon, Edwards invited us to his home without reservation, merely noting that he thought it had been an awfully long time since someone had stopped by asking about 66.

Edwards escorts us into his breezeway office, festooned with Route 66 memorabilia and piled in the corners with books and magazines. It's as much a museum as that hallway back at the Dixie Truckers Home, and Edwards is its prize exhibit. The stories come freely—hungry families with only enough money for gas, but who left with full bellies and sandwiches for later, the truckers and musicians passing back and forth. He has a thousand of them. But in nary a one will you find Ernie Edwards anywhere but behind the counter of the Pig Hip.

Standing in front of the shuttered restaurant, with old 66 behind him, Edwards recalls giving directions to a local state park, and describing its features to decades worth of travelers. "I'd never been there," he says with a hoarse laugh. "Not until after I retired, anyway."

Today, the road Ernie Edwards sunk his life into pays him back in kind. He gets a handful of tourists every week, mostly foreigners, stopping in to look at the Pig Hip and hear stories about the old days. He turns none away, and that activity is something inherently more valuable than money or fame to a man retired from such an active life.

From Many, One

We like to believe great people are different. Those who jet around the world building dams or sitting in plush offices commanding empires, we assume have stronger wills and higher IQs, better health, and more attractive children. They don't. What separates people who end up in history books from the rest of us is an obsession. Cy Avery's obsession was roads.

Cyrus Stevens Avery was born in Pennsylvania, and moved to what was then simply known as Indian Territory when he was a teen. After graduating from college he married and tried his hand at real estate and coal, and dabbled in the oil lease business with Harry Sinclair. After World War I he opened a service station and restaurant just outside of Tulsa. Now a successful businessman and community leader, Avery became involved in public service. Whether it was blind altruism or a vested interest in transportation, he found his niche in highway planning.

In 1925 Avery, who by then was an Oklahoma state highway commissioner, was appointed to the Joint Board on Interstate Highways, a federal committee convened to adopt a national highway numbering system.

"What the Joint Board was trying to do was identify the best existing roads at the time," says Richard Weingroff, a Federal Highway Administration liaison who has written widely on transportation

Long before cruise-control, drive-through windows, and rest stop vending machines, travelers relied on spots such as the Dixie Cafe for a hot meal. *Dixie Truckers Home/Illinois Route 66 Association.*

history. "Some states had adopted numbering for their own state roads, but nationally the roads had names. Everyone knew the Lincoln Highway, or the Jefferson Highway, or the Atlantic Highway or Pacific Highway; that's how they were listed on maps."

Route 66 and the entire grid wasn't so much built as it was imagined. Over the summer the Board studied maps, and traveled throughout the country getting input from local planners on how to connect the best roads.

"In some areas, the southwest in particular, there was only one way the road could go. If there was an established route through a mountain pass, for instance, you obviously weren't going to build a new one," Weingroff continues. But in some cases, the board had a number of options, and none of the commissioners were blind to the prosperity a steady stream of travelers could provide an otherwise rural area.

Next Page
Like an aircraft carrier in the middle of a cornfield, the Dixie Truckers Home hums with traffic 24 hours a day. Now operated by Mark and Kathy Beeler, the Trucker's Home also has locations in Effingham, Tuscola, and LeRoy.

The Illinois Route 66 Association operates this small museum in a back hallway of the Dixie Truckers Home. What it lacks in space, it more than makes up for in traffic at the busy truck stop.

"The equipment was gettting old, and so were we," said Ernie Edwards, of his decision to close the Pig Hip Restuarant nine years ago. He would like to see it turned into a Route 66 museum.

At the time, there were no major through-routes passing through Oklahoma, and Avery was determined to bring one home. He picked the route from Chicago to Los Angeles, and made fast friends of the highway commissioners from Missouri and Illinois, whose states would also benefit.

The main east-west intercontinental routes all had numbers that ended in zero, and Avery wanted the status and traffic a main route would bring. So the Chicago-to-Los Angeles road was designated Route 60. When the Board turned in its plan in October, Kentucky Governor William Fields was not amused.

Fields looked at the grid, and saw Route 80, 70, and 50 all stretching westward from the Atlantic. But, as he looked for Route 60, which should have started in Virginia and cut through his state, the governor was dumbstruck. Route 60 started in Chicago, hundreds of miles to the north. Fields, who had served seven terms in Congress

before becoming governor, was a well-connected man, and wouldn't go down without a fight.

Avery and his counterparts in Illinois and Missouri fought to keep the main road designation, but in the end the Joint Board saw Avery's end run for what it was, and sided with Fields. The grid was redrawn, with Route 60 now starting in Norfolk, and running in fits and starts across northern Kentucky before joining the Chicago-to-Los Angeles route, now designated Route 66, in Springfield, Missouri.

Ironically, after fighting so hard for the highway to pass through his state, Fields was voted out of office the next year after proposing a massive bond issue to improve Kentucky's infrastructure. Avery, though dubbed "The Father of Route 66" by some, was a political appointee who also left office the next year. But as Avery

"Gimme one off that there pig hip," said the farmer, pointing at a large ham on the counter. When Ernie Edwards heard that, a light went on, and the Pig Hip sandwich was born. Edwards and his wife ran the restaurant for 54 years, before retiring in 1991.

faded from the national spotlight, Route 66's reputation began to grow.

"Today, we look back with nostalgia, and think about stopping at a teepee motel or something, says Weingroff. "But if you were a motorist back then, you weren't thinking of anything other than keeping a firm grip on the wheel. In reality, Route 66 was a narrow, two-lane road that until the mid-1930s was still compacted dirt in some areas. It was very unsafe."

But before it was even completely paved, Route 66 was becoming an American icon. In the early 1930s dust storms rolled across the southern plains killing livestock and crops, and burying farms in thick layers of powdery dirt. Already strained by the hardships of the Depression, thousands of families simply packed up and left to look for a better life. For most of them, that meant California.

In 1936 *The San Francisco News* commissioned a young novelist to write a series of articles on migrant workers. John Steinbeck, whose *Tortilla Flat* had just been published to wide acclaim, filed a seven-part series called "The Harvest Gypsies" that October. But the workers, many of whom had fled the Dust Bowl on Route 66, had captured Steinbeck's imagination, and those articles became the foundation of what some consider to be his greatest work, *The Grapes of Wrath*.

No matter how many times you do it, crossing the Mississippi River always feels momentous. The flat, muddy expanse moves swiftly past St. Louis, punctuated by throws of driftwood and riverboat casinos. If Chicago is a city on the make, then St. Louis is a city on the verge. It has always chugged along dutifully, producing Chuck Berry, the occasional baseball player, and an ocean of beer, but has never quite managed to distinguish itself as a world-class city.

Route 66 took several different routes through St. Louis over the years. With a good map and a loose schedule you can wind through them, but many of the neighborhoods have deteriorated, making it both faster and safer to follow Interstate 270 around the northern edge of the city until it splits off to Highway 100 west.

Rolling out of St. Louis and into the verdant hills to the west you enter the other Missouri. Far from the ballparks and breweries, Route 66 follows the vestiges of what was once the Osage Trail. In later years telegraph lines went through, and the county highways that were stitched together into

Route 66 were known as the "Wire Road." And while you are technically headed west, a drive through central Missouri begins to feel more like a drive straight south.

What's left of the old highway is a hodge-podge of service roads and crumbling blacktop. Though you couldn't go as far as call it tree-lined, what trees remain are fine ones. Old oaks and willows line the roadway announcing tiny towns, and bird-pecked apple trees sit abandoned along the miles in between. In several places you can choose between traveling Route 66 as it was aligned in the 1930s, 1940s, or 1950s, and though the newest road is usually twice as fast, it also has half the character.

If there is a pastime here other than baseball it is the yard sale. In the middle of town, or the middle of nowhere, card tables full of used kitchenware and last year's Beanie Babies sit in front yards along the old road. Elsewhere, it seems these things last a day or two, but whether out of necessity or stubbornness, the Missouri yard sale is an all-summer event. Even if the wares come inside at night, it seems they are back in the same place the next day, and the day after that.

Shady Jack's Saloon

Nestled into a tree-lined hillside outside of Villa Ridge, Shady Jack's Saloon and Camp-Inn is a rare bird on the old road—a newcomer. While many Route 66 landmarks still thrive because of

CHAPTER 2

Missouri

Down the Old Wire Road

Route 66 cuts a long diagonal swath across southern Missouri. Just south of Springfield, an old steel bridge spans a creek full of oblivious carp.

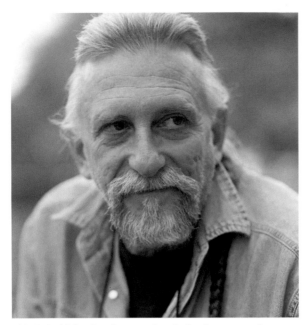

"Shady Jack" Larrison is a new breed of entrepreneur along Route 66. Although he doesn't try to capitalize on his place's proximity to the old road, he routinely fills his 20-acre campground with travelers.

Shady Jack's Saloon and Camp-Inn is the perfect rest stop for large groups of motorcyclists.

their historic connection to the highway, "Shady Jack" Larrison opened his saloon with only a vague idea of its proximity to the route.

"I never really thought about it," he says, scratching his chin and pushing an errant ponytail back over his shoulder. "I mean, I always knew this was Route 66 down here, but never thought of it as a tourist thing."

Larrison, 57, has owned two things for most of his adult life: motorcycles and bars. And while his love affair with motorcycles began in 1960, he didn't get into the bar business until 15 years later, for an unlikely reason.

"Well, um," Larrison says with a sheepish grin, "I was a cop." Recruited into the St. Louis Police intelligence unit, Larrison worked deep undercover. In the late 1960s, riding around the city on his motorcycle, long hair blowing in the breeze, Larrison was often stopped by St. Louis police officers who had no idea who he was.

"Man, I've been stopped, beat up and strip-searched," he continues. "Luckily, I would have my gun and credentials on me. I worked mostly hookers and radical groups. Sometimes they would put me inside a company to investigate. There really were no boundaries to speak of." But while the work was interesting, after 10 years in the intelligence unit, Larrison grew tired of the dual lifestyle and constant danger.

"I got tired of getting shot at, or shooting at people, " he says, looking off into the hillside. "At first I would jump on my scoot after a shoot-out and be shaking so bad I could barely ride. Then it got to the point where it became second nature. I finally said to myself, 'This is nuts.'"

Working undercover, Larrison had spent many nights in St. Louis bars and had befriended both the owners and clientele. After leaving the force he quickly found work as a bartender. From there he moved into managing, and ultimately buying failing taverns, turning them around, and selling them at a profit. At one point he owned five different bars.

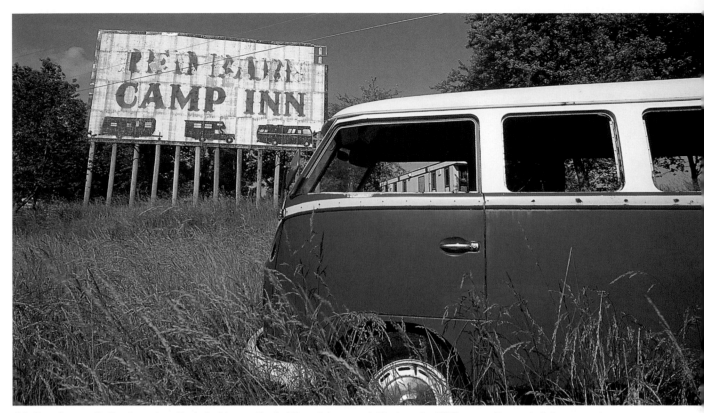

A fading sign recalls the days when Shady Jack's was the Red Barn Campground. The barn is still there, on its way to being converted into a clubhouse for visiting motorcyclists.

"I had college bars and sports bars and gay bars, but I never had a biker bar," he continues. "I had been looking for a spot for one for about two years. I was down in Daytona for Bike Week talking to a buddy about it, and he says, 'Man there's this place about 50 miles out of St. Louis—a campground.'"

The improbable biker compound he opened in 1997 has been an enormous success since its first day. Serving both the local population and biker demographic, Larrison struck on two hungry markets. Like other campgrounds, it has a full-service restaurant, bar, and swimming pool. And for the bikers there is a small shop offering Harley-Davidson merchandise and bike accessories, a leather repair service for sewing patches or mending

jackets, and a tattoo studio across the parking lot in a house trailer.

"We took an old 4x8 piece of plywood and spray-painted 'Open Tomorrow' on it, and leaned it against a pole on a Thursday afternoon," he explains. "I went into town and got 40 cases of beer and loaded them into the back of my convertible. I sold it all the first night. Actually, I ran out and had to go to Wal-Mart for more." By Monday morning Shady Jack's had become the largest beer seller in Franklin County. But his overnight success was really a function of months of hard work.

The property was originally known as the Red Barn Campground, an RV park offshoot of the

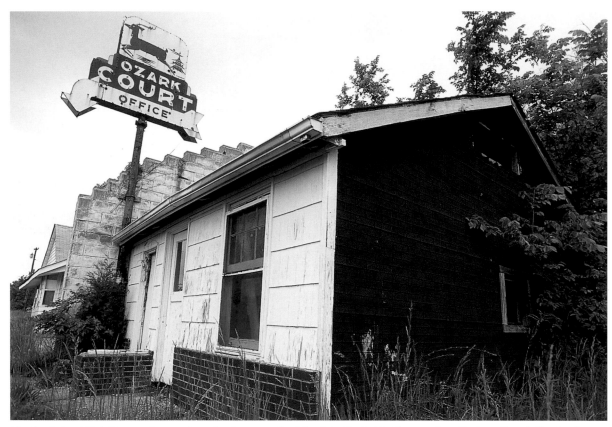

The Ozark Court Motel is one of many places to close once the interstate diverted traffic away from its door. Though the sign is no longer visible, we can only assume there is a vacancy.

Ramada Inn. Situated smack between I-44 and old Route 66, it drew a steady flow of campers and RVers before closing in 1987. The property soon became a Mecca for local teens and fly-dumpers, and before long was a wash of broken bottles and abandoned appliances.

"We hauled 27 dump loads of trash out of here. It was a pile of shit," Larrison explains. "The kids had just turned it into a big clubhouse, and other people came up here and dropped trash here too. You can imagine, being vacant for nine years, what it must have looked like.

"Actually, I didn't think we were going to make it. My brother thought I was nuts and tried to talk me out of it. But I knew this was something I

wanted to do. I really felt there was a need for it." Larrison's gut instinct was correct.

He's expanded his kitchen and is adding a meeting room off the pool area, a banquet hall upstairs, and is planning to renovate a barn into a clubhouse. He routinely fills the 20-acre campground with motorcycle and hot rod clubs, as well as veterans groups and the occasional Native American powwow. Though local bankers were skeptical when he first came to town, they've learned to respect his success and business savvy.

"When I first walked into the bank to buy this place, they looked at me like I had two heads. But after about a year and a half of going in there every three months with my profit and loss statements,

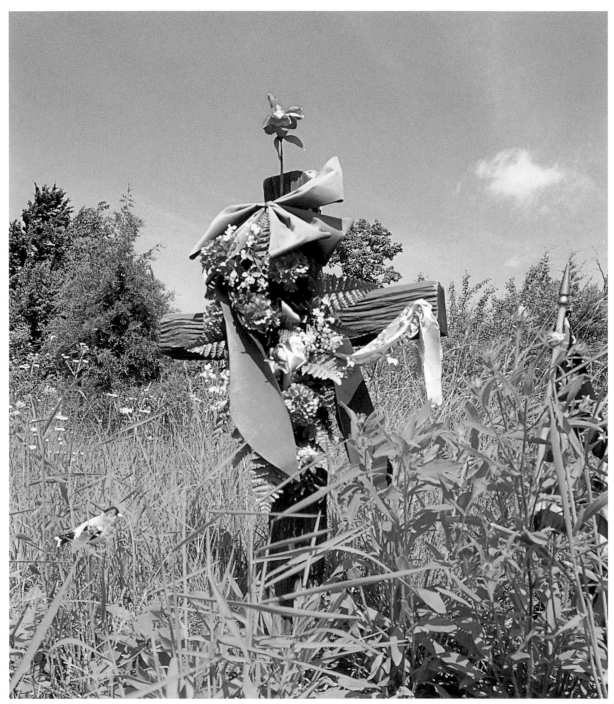

While we romanticize it today, in its infancy Route 66 was a very dangerous road, earning the nickname "Bloody 66" for obvious reasons. Even with speed limits and seat belts, the old road still claims its share of lives, as evidenced by this roadside cross outside Cuba.

Yard sales spring up everywhere along the road throughout southern Missouri. If the rust is any indication, this one in Carthage has a tough time moving inventory.

they started realizing I knew what I was doing. Hell, the banker comes out here every once in a while to visit."

Shady Jack navigates the turns through the kitchen and out behind the bar in long, fluid strides. Whether the product of years on a motorcycle or those spent dodging bullets, his cat-like moves mirror his easygoing manner.

His saloon has become different things to different people. To the locals it's a neighborhood tavern and restaurant. To the bikers it's a place to have club meetings and conventions—a place where they will be both respected and left alone. To the bank, it's a raucous reminder that men in suits are not the only ones with a flair for business. For

Route 66 travelers, especially those on motorcycles, it is a new and welcome oasis away from the urban grit of St. Louis. And for Jack Larrison, it is a dream come true.

He would like to open a chain of similar campgrounds throughout the country, and already has his eye on a location farther south in Missouri, in the Ozarks. But while he continues to plan for the future, Larrison remains pragmatic about the nature of business.

"I've been lucky," he says. "It takes money to run these joints, and you have to have money you're willing to lose. When I bought this place I had just gotten a divorce and didn't have the kind of money I needed to keep it going. I figured if I

The last major town before entering Kansas, Joplin's main drag is mostly deserted on an early Saturday night. The steak houses on the edge of town are standing room only, however.

would try it and if it all collapsed, I'd just get on my scoot and leave. And I feel the same way today. One of these days I'm going to hand this place over to my son and jump on my scoot and go. There's always something else going on down the road."

Bloody 66

There are many things you'll see a lot of along this stretch of Route 66, but two seem to pop up with an eerie regularity: abandoned motels and roughly hewn handmade crosses.

The motels pop up every few miles, closer together than one would think the laws of supply and demand could accommodate. Perhaps that played a part in their demise, but a more obvious reason lies a few hundred yards away: Interstate 44. When it came through the old highway was relegated to use as an access road and the steady stream of travelers who once filled the rooms now sped by without even noticing the roadside inns.

The tradition of placing a decorated cross along the road where someone died is practiced nationally, but this stretch of the old road seems to have more than its fair share. Either folks here are mighty diligent about keeping them up, or "Bloody 66" has yet to live down its reputation.

They come in all shapes and sizes, but are typically around two feet tall and decorated with wildflowers. You'll notice them along the roadside in the middle of nowhere, tucked into the tall ditch grass or set out next to a mailbox. The newest ones are easy to discern, the vibrant purple and white flowers standing out against the green roadside. And while the sight of a new cross might cause you to ease up on that accelerator just a bit, realizing there are also two older ones next to it will bring you to a full stop.

As it continues west, Route 66 dips slowly south into the Ozark foothills. Signs for tourist attractions such as Meramec Caverns near Stanton, or the many wineries in the area dot the sides of the road. Running almost diagonally through Rolla, Lebanon, Springfield, and on through Joplin, the land begins to flatten back out. Lush hills recede into cornfields.

Crossing the border from Missouri into Kansas feels for all the world like sneaking in the back entrance of something. After bumping along the old road for a mile or so you climb a crumbling overpass and see what is left of the mining town of Galena.

There are still piles of mine waste, known as slag or chat, piled here and there a few hundred yards from the road. The town, like its country cousin in Illinois, was named for the type of ore that yielded tons of lead and a trickle of silver. But while its northern counterpart has evolved into a trendy tourist destination, Galena, Kansas, has faded quietly into oblivion. Driving through town early in the morning it's hard to tell which of the storefronts on Main Street are closed for the day, or closed for good.

Ahead in Riverton, the Eisler Brothers' General Store is the headquarters of all things Route 66 for the state of Kansas. Scott Nelson, its proprietor, runs the Kansas Route 66 Association, and the store's relaxed charm makes it a regular stop for those driving the road. It's a sunny but breezy morning when we pull into the Eislers' lot, and the place is absolutely buzzing. A

CHAPTER 3

Kansas

The Few, The Proud

group of German tourists traveling Route 66 on motorcycles from L.A. to Chicago is encamped for coffee and pastry. They're a motley bunch, all lawyers and junior vice-presidents, but their enthusiasm for Route 66 is innocent, almost childlike, and infectious.

Just west of Riverton, the Marsh Arch Bridge spans Brush Creek. Built in 1923, it's the newest and last survivor in a series of concrete arch bridges that were built within a few miles of one other. Once covered in graffiti, its fresh coat of white paint is still serviceable, although a few Route 66 travelers have written their names along the span.

There never was much of Route 66 in Kansas, just over 13 miles at best. While many towns grimaced as interstates bypassed them, Kansas bears the distinction of being the only state completely cut off by the closure of 66. Perhaps for that reason folks here seem to value their connection to Route 66 even more.

A handful of miles past Brush Creek is the last stop in Kansas, Baxter Springs. Though it started off as a wide-open frontier cow-town, it ultimately became famous as a tourist stop—presumably because of the healing qualities of the water from its namesake spring—long after the cattle drives ended.

Golden Years

When Route 66 was finally paved all the way to Los Angeles, there were celebrations on both ends of

There isn't much of Route 66 in Kansas, but the few miles that pass through the Sunflower State are lovingly tended by a dedicated group of enthusiasts. This logo painted on the pavement just over the state line is just one example.

The Eisler Brothers' General Store is a popular stopping-off point for folks traveling the length of the old highway. They come from either direction, at all hours of the day, and are always met with a smile and a cup of good Kansas coffee.

the road. But in the height of the Depression, with a black cloud of dust choking the Southwest, the first people to travel the road were driven more often by desperation than a sense of adventure.

When John Steinbeck wrote *The Grapes of Wrath*, his stark portrait of an Oklahoma family's passage to California forever tinged Route 66 with a streak of sadness. Woody Guthrie's ballads and talking blues, while often tongue-in-cheek and optimistic overall, portrayed the fate of Okies along 66 as honestly. Between the two of them, they managed to imbue Route 66 with a tinge of loss that has forever become part of its myth and allure.

As the Great Depression wound down, Hitler's war machine wound up. When the United States

A simple sign pays tribute to the 13.2 miles of Route 66 that passed through Kansas in the old days. Though there were once three similar spans in the immediate area, the Marsh Arch Bridge is the last of its type left.

entered World War II, gasoline was rationed, new tires were hard to come by, and there were as many hitchhikers as drivers on 66. But by war's end the economy had fully recovered from the Depression. Returning GIs were buying homes and cars and having families as fast as they could manufacture cribs and Oldsmobiles.

One of those returning servicemen was an aspiring singer-songwriter from Harrisburg, Pennsylvania, named Robert Troup Jr. On a driving trip to Los Angeles in the 1940s, his wife leaned over to him and whispered "get your kicks on Route 66". The phrase stuck with him. Five days after arriving in Los Angeles, Troup played the completed song to Nat King Cole. Neither Troup, nor Cole, nor Route 66 would ever be the same again.

While Cole had the biggest hit with the song, it has been recorded by every stripe of musical act, from the gutbucket blues of the early Rolling Stones to the techno-pop of Depeche Mode. Unwittingly, Troup composed an anthem that even after his death, continues to teach a nation about the joys of the "highway that's the best."

There is something disquieting about crossing the state line into Oklahoma. You notice it in your gut like a falling barometer at the first sight of road kill armadillo. This has always been wild land, whether in the possession of the Cherokee, Dust Bowl, or oil baron. And while it might be nothing more than the fine red clay soil blowing in the wind, there is still a taste of frontier in the air.

Unlike Kansas, there is a whole lot of Route 66 in Oklahoma, and a whole lot of Oklahoma in Route 66. The old road cuts a long, diagonal path across the state, dipping through Tulsa and Oklahoma City, on through Clinton and Elk City, before entering Texas just west of Texola.

It is here in the northeast corner of Oklahoma that history begins to come alive along Route 66. As you pass through Commerce, Miami, and Narcissa, you get a clearer sense of what the road was probably like in its glory days. Though these rural communities are obviously not all they once were, it seems that day-to-day life has remained fundamentally the same over the years.

When Route 66 was first paved in this part of the country, the roadbed was only nine feet wide,

CHAPTER 4

Oklahoma

Barbecue for Breakfast

including the concrete curbs. While the course of the highway changed a few years later, a few miles of these original sections are still drivable. Finding them, however, is a different matter. The maps and books we carry all place these sections somewhere between Miami and Afton. Upon reaching Afton without finding any sign of the original roadbed, we stop into the Route 66 Diner for a cup of coffee. Once sated with fresh pie and hot joe, we ask the waitress if she knows anyone around town familiar with the history of Route 66.

"What was you wantin' to know?" she asks. After explaining what we are doing, and what we are looking for, she sets the coffee pot down on our table and says with a smile, "Let me tell ya a little story."

Her father had worked on the crews that paved the road back in 1926. In a few minutes she gives us a thumbnail history and directions back to where some of the original alignment is still visible. We backtrack out of town, and turn off the state road. The road is rough but passable, quaint but unremarkable. We follow it along for a while, assuming we missed our turn-off again and are headed down just another Oklahoma gravel road. Then I see it.

A thin line of concrete begins to peek up through the clay and gravel in front of the passenger side tire. A little farther along, a matching strip of concrete pokes through on the driver's side. We stop the van and get out to investigate. Those two lines are actually the curbs from the original alignment we have been seeking.

Once an oddball gift to an intended bride, the Blue Whale swimming hole attraction near Catoosa has received a fresh coat of paint and had its hat restored. While passé to the locals, travelers are often startled by the behemoth in the middle of nowhere.

In Miami (pronounced My-am-uh in these parts), the Coleman Theater has gone through years of wavering business and states of repair. These days, though not all it once was, the old movie house is the pride of downtown.

A nine-foot-wide section—complete with curbs—of the original Route 66 roadbed near Afton. Legend has it that officials only paved it half as wide a necessary so they could go twice as far with the same money.

After a few hundred yards the full road emerges out of the gravel. Though pockmarked and bumpy, it is in remarkable shape given its age. We get out to take a closer look, keeping a close watch on the darkening western sky.

A series of tornadoes has just pummeled the area south and west of here a few days before, and both of us have seen enough PBS specials to know that although bad storms hit everywhere, they hit Oklahoma first and worst. The dark patch grows closer, as the temperature drops, and we barely manage to get the gear stowed before it hits the fan.

The wind blows hard enough to toss me against the side of the van, and the sky turns so black that headlights provide little relief. Rain pounds us in waves as we hurry back to the state highway. We speed south as fast as we can, and come out the other side of the front just south of Vinita.

Just outside Sapulpa, this old brick bed bridge is one of the few spots along the road where Route 66 and Old Route 66 are so marked.

Inside the Greenwood Cultural Center in Tulsa, there are stunning displays showing the history of what was known as Black Wall Street, a thriving business section. Home to the Oklahoma Jazz Hall of Fame, the walls are lined with historic photographs and artwork.

By the time we pass Catoosa it is a sunny afternoon with no hint of the storm that had just come through. Rolling into Tulsa to look for a motel, we spot a flag salesman near the side of the road. The flags are all Confederate, Nazi, or combinations of each.

Oklahoma has seen its share of good and bad over the years, and bears a grim distinction in the United States. The two greatest instances of Americans killing fellow Americans outside of the Civil War both happened here: when Timothy McVeigh parked

Outside the Greenwood Cultural Center, a somber marker bears witness to the Tulsa race riots of 1921. Whites stormed the neighborhood, killing more than 300, burning 36 square blocks, and herding more than 6,000 people into a nearby stadium. Recent investigations have discovered mass graves in the area that may push the number of dead even higher.

The Rock Café in Stroud was long a favorite stop for Route 66 travelers.

a rental truck outside the Murrah Federal Building in Oklahoma City in 1995, and when Ku Klux Klansmen burned 36 square blocks in the Greenwood district of Tulsa in 1921, killing more than 300 people.

There are two main museums dedicated to Route 66 in Oklahoma. The National Route 66 Museum in Elk City is modeled after a small town, replete with General Store, one-room schoolhouse, and towering Kachina statue. Spread across a few acres on the west edge of town, it's hard to miss. But for all its hokey theme park charm, the national museum rates a close second to its country cousin back in Clinton.

The Oklahoma Route 66 Museum is a neon and polished steel beauty. Visitors are given a portable cassette player and headphones, which provides a narrated tour they take at their own pace. Divided by decade, the exhibits range from the sober (an ancient flatbed Ford truck piled high with a Dustbowl family's possessions), to the psy-

chedelic (a Day-Glo-painted and black light-lit Volkswagen van from the 1960s). And while the museum is loaded to the rafters with interesting artifacts, across the street is a slice of Americana every bit as kitschy and compelling as Route 66.

Like a lot of things along the old road, the Best Western motel used to be something else. Back in the 1960s when it was the Gold Crown, the little motel in Clinton played host to a very famous visitor: Elvis Presley. He would usually arrive around midnight, on his way to or from Las Vegas, and spend most of the next day sleeping. Though he

Next Page
Long after an explosion ripped through the Murrah Federal Building in Oklahoma City, a statue of Christ was erected across the street. Back turned to the site of the tragedy, face in his hand, the inscription simply reads: "And Jesus Wept." Note the missing roof of the building in the background, yet to be replaced after being blown off in the bombing.

Lucille Hamon's gas station near Hydro was a mainstay along Route 66 for over 50 years. Although she passed away in 2000, pilgrims still stop to stare in her windows and reflect at the simple cross memorial to the "Mother of the Mother Road."

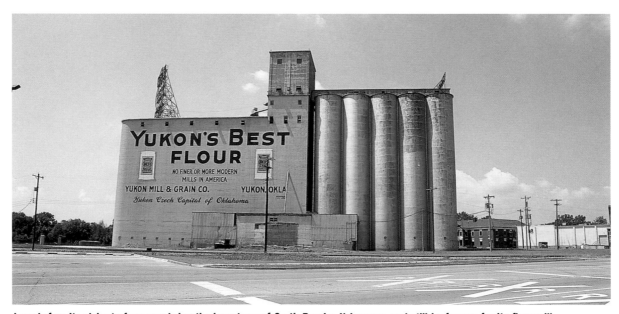

Long before its claim to fame was being the hometown of Garth Brooks, Yukon was, and still is, famous for its flour mill.

An old pickup sits silently on display at the Oklahoma Route 66 Museum in Clinton. Inside, visitors can view the history of the old road by decade, from the humble possessions of a Dust Bowl family to the psychedelic Volkswagen of latter-day refugees.

stayed there four times over the course of the years, the staff and townspeople only saw him once.

A housekeeper recognized Presley when she delivered his room service meal and spread the word through town. In short time a crowd gathered outside, waiting to get a peek at the entertainer. He eventually emerged to sign autographs and chat with the crowd, even pausing to play ball with some of the children in the parking lot. But soon, when his entourage had the bus loaded, he waved good-bye and drove off.

The room Presley stayed in is still there, carefully preserved with the same furniture and fixtures as the mid-1960s. It's available for a small premium above standard rates, a small price for a room fit for The King.

A Child of the Mother Road

Though he makes his home in Tennessee these days, songwriter Kevin Welch's ties to Oklahoma and Route 66 run deep. He grew up traveling the old highway with his family and eventually settled near it in Tulsa in 1962.

Like most young southern men with ambitions and a guitar, Welch left Tulsa and migrated to

Elvis Presley passed through Clinton a number of times, always staying at the Golden Crown Motel on Route 66. Though today it is owned by the Best Western chain, Presley's room is preserved exactly as it was in the 1960s, when the singer last stayed there.

Nashville to pursue a music career. He found success as a songwriter, penning hits for country superstars such as Waylon Jennings, Roger Miller, and Ricky Skaggs. And all the while he was writing songs for others, Welch was building a potent portfolio of songs for himself.

In 1990, he released his major label debut, simply titled *Kevin Welch*. Its amalgam of punchy songwriting and twangy arrangements kept it from fitting easily into the playlists of rock or country radio, yet critics everywhere applauded Welch's undiluted style. One of the tracks contained was a paean to Route 66, simply titled, "The Mother Road." Though never released as a single, the song soon became something of an anthem for Route 66 enthusiasts and Americana buffs in general. And if there was any question about his sincerity or connection to the road, Welch explains it best in his own words:

"I was born in 1955 in Long Beach, California, where Dad was working as an aircraft mechanic. In those days, his job involved contract work with a field team of other mechanics, doing maintenance or modifications to any number of different type aircraft, usually for some branch of the military. Once a contract was fulfilled, the entire crew, including families, would pack up and move caravan style to the next job. This would typically mean driving from one side of the country to the other. Once we had arrived, everyone would set up housekeeping as best they could until the time came to move out again.

"Naturally, traveling as much as we did in those days involved many, many miles on old Route 66. I remember canvas bags of water hanging in front of the radiator for the long pulls across the desert. I learned to read from highway signs and billboards. The first real book of rules I learned was highway-driving etiquette, and I admired the truck drivers and their skills as much as my dad did. All of my earliest memories are of the road: the gas stations (especially the red flying horse); the curio shops; fighting with my little brother in the back seat; or even, when I was real small, before David had arrived, riding on the floorboard of one of the pickup trucks we had for a while; or sleeping up behind the back seat below the rear window, a favorite spot.

"When we finally stopped moving, we settled just a few miles south of Route 66, close to the mighty intersection of I-40 and I-35. I will never forget my dad driving me down Sooner Road to where 66 crossed it, and telling me that if I went left, I could get to California, and if I went right, I could get to Chicago. I was 7 years old, and knowing that made me feel that I had the power and the freedom of any grown-up anywhere. It was nice to stop moving, but I felt so much more secure knowing how easy it would be to go back to the old ways. I lasted 10 years, leaving home to travel again at 17. Ever since, I have felt truly comfortable only when in motion.

"Back in those days, to my family, a road was a road, and it was judged based on its condition. So it's significant to me that even with those criteria, Route 66 still meant something more to us. It has always been a big deal to me, further back than my conscious mind remembers. I guess, as a child, I assumed the specialness of it was a secret only we were aware of. In later years, I was surprised and pleased that others felt the same way, particularly those who still live on the road. I was glad to learn they didn't take it for granted, and that they remembered its importance and history. Back in those days I thought of it as one very long, very thin city, and the ones who traveled it habitually as its residents. It was as much a hometown as anywhere else for us.

"Over the years I tried time and time again to express all this. I had dozens of bits and pieces of songs that never went anywhere. It was too big to say in a song. Too much of my own make-up was involved, and a song is such a tiny thing to jam a life into. Then one day my friend

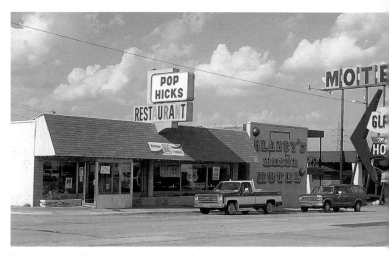

For years, Pop Hicks' restaurant was a favorite with Clinton locals and Route 66 travelers. Sadly, the business was destroyed after an electrical fire in 1999. There are no plans to rebuild.

Jonathan Lee Pickens stopped off at my house and told me about a newscast he had just seen. They said that the last stretch of the old road had finally been bypassed, out in Arizona, I think, or maybe New Mexico. It was a strange piece of news to hear. He had an idea for a song title, based on John Steinbeck's name for it, 'The Children of the Mother Road.' I was, I think, a little stunned by it all.

"That day or the next, Alan Rhody and I started a writing appointment, a common practice back then, as we were both staff writers for a large publishing company. The only thing on my mind was this story, and I told him about it. I dragged out all the notes I had kept for all those years and added them to the stack of words I already had. Alan wrote many of the key lines for the song, and soon we had finished 'Children of the Mother Road.' It still seemed, and still does, like only a tiny drop in the bucket. I always assumed I would write more songs to add to it, and really never have, unless you count all the many songs involving travel I've written since.

MYRTLE
KACHINA DOLL

"In all the hypnotic rush of research and creation, my friend Jon Pickens, a tremendous songwriter, was completely left out of the process, and I have never stopped kicking my ass for that. I still am looking for a way to make that right with him, and someday I will.

"I've told some of this story before, but never in writing, and I just thought it best that you understood that I'm not playing around here when I sing that song. It doesn't come from anywhere but my own life, and to some extent, it *is* my life. They say the first seven years of a child's life are the formative ones, and I have reason to believe they may be right. It's a tender subject. I'm just one of millions whose lives have been affected by Route 66, and mine are small stories compared to some, but I thank you for the chance to tell some of them."

The Sword of Damocles

Things had more of an air of permanence about them in the 1950s. It was possible, almost expected, that you would find a good job and stay at it until you retired. That corner drug store had been there as long as you could remember and would be there long after you stopped concerning yourself with it. Before streamlined chain operations began slouching into rural communities and driving the locals out of business, you could count on things to last.

Legend has it that President Eisenhower was so impressed by Germany's autobahn, he felt the United States. should have a comparable system. While Ike might have liked a good drive as much as the next president, he had more pragmatic reasons for

The god Kachina Kaubat is revered in Native American culture and is a familiar sight along Route 66. This statue stands outside the National Route 66 Museum in Elk City.

Jobe's Charburgers is one of hundreds of businesses who advertise their historic connection to the old road.

wanting to upgrade our highways. As a general he knew a quick system for moving troops and equipment between coasts was an essential part of national defense, and post-Korea, with the Cold War beginning to simmer, national defense wasn't far from people's minds. Although the superhighways were intended to move troops and equipment, an urban legend ultimately circulated that the government ordered one mile in five be straight, for use as emergency landing strips.

There will always be the folksingers among us who, regardless of what piece of progress and modernity confronts them, will feel the need to launch into a few bars about how good the old one was. Interstates weren't and aren't evil in and of themselves. In fact, the newer, faster roads did

much to increase the popularity of the driving vacation. But as Newton warned, "for every action, there is an equal and opposite reaction."

As the four-lane roads began skirting the edges of small towns all along Route 66, local businesses scrambled to attract customers. The savvier merchants quickly bought property near the exchanges and moved out to where they stood a chance of catching a few travelers' dollars. But for many small gas stations and restaurants, it meant a slow, agonizing death. While the long-haul truckers and vacationing families who once passed through their towns now sped happily by on the interstate, all along the old road stores closed, "for sale" signs went up, and the owners of the few that survived went home to an increasingly taller stack of unpaid bills.

We do. And for a couple of city boys who spend a good portion of their week in rush hour traffic, all this friendly waving and folks getting out of your way to let you pass feels a bit foreign. In the brown north country of Texas, the state measures less than 200 miles across. Here in the panhandle it's dusty, hot, and unforgiving, and if there is a redeeming quality about the landscape, it is only that it is not New Mexico or Arizona, exponentially wider and twice as hot.

The small brick service station outside Alanreed is overgrown but not crumbling. The hand-cut wood sign attached to the front reads "Super 66 Service Station." Peering inside, it looks as if someone simply turned the key and walked away, albeit many years before. A small desk still has paperwork on it; the nub of a pencil lies tossed to the side. In the opposite corner, a simple pallet bed still has its pillow and roughly sewn quilt, and next to it is a potbelly stove that has been cold for decades. The windows are covered with greasy dust, and on them fellow travelers have written

their initials and the dates of their visits. We add ours between "Tom 4/10/99," and "Soon Jung Kwang 1998-10."

Once a thriving business, the old station is now an exhibit, on display for those traveling the living museum that Route 66 has become. Though its function has given way to form, it is in many ways a piece of public art—there for anyone to see and interpret through his or her own experiential filters. And while we tend to associate public art with statues and murals in exotic locations, this stretch of old Route 66 has several examples of outdoor art, from the serious to the comic. The next one is just outside the town of Groom.

It is billed as the largest cross in North America, and even from a mile out that claim seems reasonable. The religious behemoth is visible from both Route 66 and I-40 to the north, positioned that way to beam its message to locals and travelers alike. Though the cross itself is rather modern looking, at its base there are more traditional life-sized statues of Christ at the Stations of the Cross. Though many people only see it from the interstate at 70 miles per hour, the lot is just as often full of tour busses and traveling families who can't pass up the curiosity.

Though the cross and its underlying message are an integral part of the way American culture has shaped itself over the years, a few clicks farther up the road is something just as American, without the serious undertones.

CHAPTER 5

Texas

Drive Friendly

Local millionaire Stanley Marsh 3 conspired with an avant-garde art collective known as the Ant Farm to produce the classic bit of Americana: Cadillac Ranch. Though locals are either hot or cold on this and other Marsh projects, the Ranch is instantly recognizable by people from around the world.

The leaning water tower outside Britten might have been inspired by a certain structure in Pisa, Italy, but its mission is good old-fashioned American huckstering. Designed to attract both attention and visitors to Britten, travelers have indeed done double takes as they passed into town. Whether they actually stopped and patronized any of the local merchants as town fathers intended is unclear, but the tower remains one of those classic, funky treasures along Route 66.

The leaning tower and giant cross are fine examples of unintentional public art. At the core, they are advertisements, selling religion and civic pride with equal fervor. Whatever artistic merit they have is secondary, noted more by latter-day observers and critics than through the intentions of the people who erected them. But a few miles up the road there is art to be found that is both intentional and serious-minded.

The area surrounding Amarillo is one of the richest helium fields in the world. While a lot of Texas fortunes were built on oil, up here they're built on gas. Stanley Marsh 3 (as opposed to the more traditional III) is a helium man, prankster, and a visionary with a passion for art.

In certain circles you can't swing a cat without hitting a person willing to explain *ad infinatum* the artistic relevance of Marsh's Cadillac Ranch. But mostly what you are struck by as you trek up the compacted dirt road that leads to it is the realization that someone has stuck a bunch of cars into the ground nose first.

Yet no matter how haphazard it looks, Marsh's world-renowned installation on the western edge of Amarillo has broader themes behind it. The 10 Cadillacs, from a 1949 Coupe to a 1963 sedan, are buried in a simple line at the same angle as the Pyramid of Cheops in Egypt. When the Ranch was

In what was once downtown Alanreed, Bradley Kiser's old Super 66 Service Station is now a landmark for Route 66 travelers, who leave their initials written on the dusty windows after viewing the period interior.

originally installed in 1974, the outskirts of Amarillo were still miles away. But over the years, development crept west. By early 1997, several mega-stores and (ironically) a Cadillac dealership had become neighbors. Marsh was not pleased with his work's new backdrop. That August he brought in heavy equipment and moved the whole installation two miles down the road, telling local reporters that the cars had wanted to enter a square dance contest.

Over the years it has become a tradition for locals and tourists alike to leave their names and words of wisdom inscribed somewhere on the cars, making it a truly interactive art exhibit. It is rumored Marsh stops by periodically and watches people's reactions, often chatting with them without ever revealing his connection to the work. But while the Cadillac Ranch leans toward the whimsical, another bit of Marsh's handiwork is more rooted in serious literature.

A few miles south of town, what appears to be a broken statue sits unnoticed by travelers whizzing by on the nearby interstate. But "them legs" as it was called by a local merchant from whom we asked directions is in reality titled *Ozymandias*, a serious spot of art inspired by the great Romantic poet Percy Bysshe Shelley.

Written in 1818, *Ozymandias* is one of Shelley's most-beloved sonnets. The title comes from the Greek name for Ramses II, the Pharaoh that Moses and the Israelites fled long before the birth of Christ. The poem tells the story of a traveler who encounters a crumbling statue of the Pharaoh while exploring the Egyptian desert:

> *I met a traveler from an antique land*
> *Who said: "Two vast and trunkless legs of stone*
> *stand in the desert."*

Some 170 years later, Marsh used Shelley's imagery as the basis for the piece, which is literally two legs on a pedestal. Like Cadillac Ranch, locals either scratch their heads in disbelief or greet it with open hostility. And every few years, when Marsh announces his intentions for another project, a good portion of Amarillo rolls its eyes with a "here we go again" sigh.

But many of his neighbors don't realize that Marsh is a subversive genius. Even if they are saying how much they hate one of his pieces, he has them talking about art. In a city with a higher incidence of bar fights than ballet performances, that's no small feat.

The Castle on Sixth Avenue

As Route 66 snakes along Sixth Avenue in Amarillo, it passes through a burgeoning antique district. Old storefronts of every stripe have been converted into consignment shops filled with the good, the bad, and the overpriced. And in the middle of it all, an interesting looking old building with a historical marker in front has a thousand stories to tell, of presidents and pop stars, travelers and Texans alike.

Before air conditioning and the $9.99 electric fan, escaping the brutal Texas heat was a welcome treat. The Amarillo Natatorium opened in July 1922 as a lavish open-air swimming pool. It was covered a year later to provide year-round use. In 1926 it was sold, and a floor was built across the drained pool, converting it into a dance hall. Patrons paid a nickel per dance, and the floor was cleared after each song.

In 1935, a restaurant was added to the north face of the building, providing an entrance from Route 66, and business boomed. The ballroom soon became a regular venue for MCA orchestras passing through Amarillo. In its prime the Nat hosted Duke Ellington, Bob Wills and his Texas Playboys, Tommy and Jimmy Dorsey, Guy Lombardo, and many others. It was also a favorite spot for private and political functions.

"It was the biggest nightclub between Dallas and Denver," says owner Pete Elkins. Though they still operate the old ballroom as an antique mall, Elkins and his business partner, Mike Baker, are determined to revive the Nat's proud history as a venue for live music. And with more than 20,000 square feet of inventory, that's not an easy task. Every night they have music, Elkins must clear the floor of all the antique displays to make room for the crowds.

"We have a whole crew that comes in," Elkins explains in an easy drawl. "We move everything out of the way and cover it all up to make room for the dancers." And while that seems like a Herculean task, Elkins shrugs it off with a football analogy.

"Shoot, man," he laughs. "They do the same thing every year at the Super Bowl. They set up a whole sound stage and everything in 15 minutes. It ain't that bad."

Over the years the Nat has played host to thousands of bands and even more patrons. Back

Like sideshow barkers, towns along Route 66 often build oddities hoping travelers would be intrigued enough to investigate, and perhaps stay long enough to drop a few dollars. Outside Britten, the leaning water tower produces more smiles than dollars.

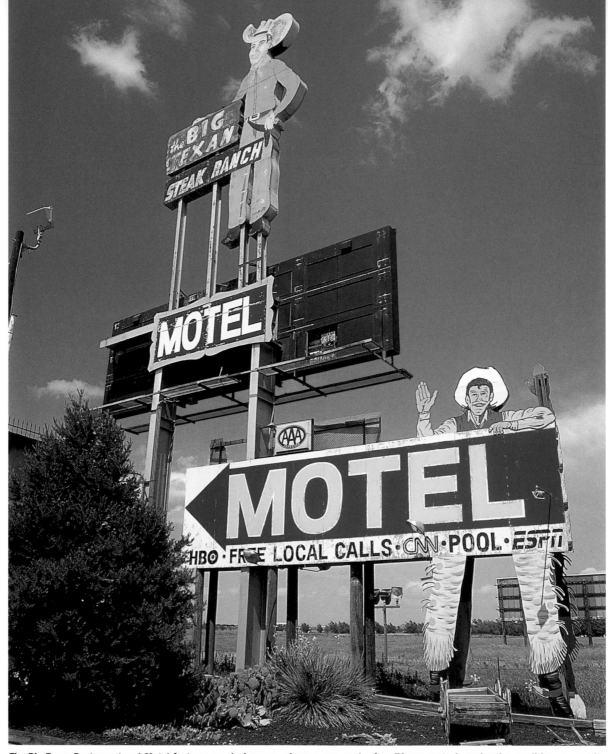

The Big Texan Restaurant and Motel features musical revues, clean rooms, and a free 72-ounce steak, under the condition you eat it and the accompanying side dishes within an hour. Few attempt it, and fewer leave without paying.

When an actual Cadillac dealership sprung up in the background of his artwork, Stanley Marsh dug up the Ranch and moved it a few miles father down the road to its current home west of Amarillo.

The Amarillo Natatorium has served as a swimming pool, a dance hall, and antique mall over the years. These days, owners continue to stock antiques, with hopes of returning the sprawling building to its roots as a dance hall.

in the 1940s it was a favorite haunt of local servicemen stationed nearby. And while there was always the occasional fight or trouble, Elkins only recalls one instance when a performer was hauled off the stage and arrested.

"Well it was back in the '50s. You have to remember now, this was a pretty redneck part of the country back then," Elkins says. "Little Richard was playing here, and I guess they said he was a little intoxicated or something. But anyway he undid a button on his shirt or something and they came and took him away."

For the record, Little Richard bothered a lot more people than just the Amarillo police back then. He raised eyebrows across the country with his sexually charged music and androgynous look, and his propensity for dropping his trousers in the middle of a performance didn't endear him to many local constabularies. Like The Doors a decade later, there were often police officers in the audience wherever he played, waiting for him to cross the line.

While Elkins features live music as much as he can, he's also set up a small broadcasting museum in a corner of the old ballroom, and a makeshift diorama saluting the Big Band era on the stage. And while he is keenly aware of the historic value of the building—it's on both the national and state register of historic deeds—there are plenty of visitors coming through that remind him.

"We get folks coming in all the time who tell me they used to dance here when they were younger," he continues. "Either that or this is the place they met their wives or husbands or something like that." In addition, the sprawling complex is something of a time capsule. Elkins says he is forever turning up old ticket stubs and photos from under a carpet or behind a wall.

Wipe the windows, check the oil, dollar gas. A long-closed Glen Rio gas station still has cars waiting out front for service that will never come.

Although he doesn't stock much, if anything, in the way of Route 66 souvenirs, Elkins says he gets a steady stream of people in his shop who are traveling the old road. "The local Route 66 association has done a lot to help turn this area around," he explains. "We have all sorts of events, and book signings and so forth."

Walking along the creaky wooden floors in the old swimming hole *cum* dance hall, it's easy to imagine the place full of flirting couples and sweating musicians. Like so many places along the old road, the Nat is full of ghosts. We take our leave of Amarillo, on our way to a place where the ghosts outnumber the living.

Glen Rio's Relics

West of Amarillo it is flat, flatter, flattest. Old Route 66, now a bumpy access road, runs parallel with I-40 for a good spell, so there is little difference between driving it and the interstate. Rolling ever westward through Vega and Adrian, you draw ever closer to a chilling example of what happened to hundreds of towns when traffic was routed off of Route 66 and onto the interstate.

There never was much of Glen Rio, which shows up on maps in New Mexico as often as it does Texas. There is a house at either end of town with laundry on the line, and pickup trucks too new to be abandoned in their driveways. But what lies between is every bit the ghost town it's advertised to be.

Even in the blazing sun of a Texas summer, Glen Rio is an unsettling place. Things are uncertain and often contradictory here. Though dead as a town can be, the place buzzes with life. Gophers scurry across your boots in the overgrown yards, while grasshoppers thrum all around, almost drowning out the interstate, and a pack of stray dogs arrogantly roams the main drag.

Rusting cars sit in front of an overgrown gas station, as if waiting for service. An occasional car passes through headed west, but invariably returns

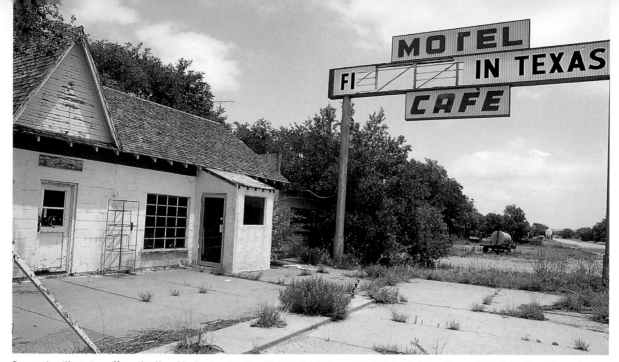

Once a bustling stop off on the New Mexico border, the First Motel in Texas/Last Motel in Texas is a rotting hulk. Though much of the building has been stripped of usable items, the combination motel, gas station, and diner's banking and business records lie among the ruins for all to see.

a few minutes later, afraid to try the primitive road leading west out of town. It is both a symbolic and literal end of the road. None but the brave or local rancher passes through Glen Rio without hurrying quickly back from whence they came.

Just down the street is the shell of what was once Glen Rio's finest business. Depending which way you are headed, the sign in front reads either Last Motel in Texas, or First Motel in Texas. Aside from people traveling Route 66, its only regular visitor these days seems to be the postal carrier, servicing the small cluster of mailboxes mounted on a pole in the building's gravel turnout.

The ruins of the old business are scattered with history. Leaning down to pick up a stack of papers, something larger than an insect darts away a few feet from my hand. Leafing through the tattered papers I realize they are the old bank records from the motel. After a little scanning and some quick math, it's obvious this was an incredibly successful place, doing a five-figure business more

than 40 years ago, and that makes the crumbling skeleton it has become even more poignant.

If nowhere else along the old road, here in Glen Rio you feel the full effect of the tragedy that must have visited thousands of other businesses when Route 66 was decommissioned. The hum of the interstate, hardly noticed before, seems louder and oddly menacing as I walk through the abandoned motel rooms and restaurant.

In front of a room near the motel office, a broken metal chair sits beside the gaping hole where a door used to be. I sit down carefully, lean back and light a cigarette, listening to the 18-wheelers screaming from the interstate a mile or so away.

Glen Rio is an odd portal in many ways. Somewhere on that short strip of blacktop you pass from Texas into New Mexico, from Central to Mountain time and from the bones of an old town into the great wide open. Pictures taken and equipment repacked, we ease the van out of the parking lot of The Last Motel in Texas in dead silence.

The road west out of Glen Rio looks questionable. Our guidebooks say it is drivable, "weather permitting," and since it's a glorious summer afternoon it seems worth a shot. The blacktop soon gives way to primitive gravel, and we descend in earnest into the *Llano estacado*, the staked plain, so named when the first settlers who passed through pounded stakes into the ground to mark a trail.

I-40 falls farther away to the north and the countryside is still, except for distant chattering of crows and mooing cattle. A huge bird—a hawk or golden eagle perhaps—rises out of an overgrown ditch as we approach. The rolling hills and crested buttes seem to announce we have officially left Texas and entered the Southwest. It's almost 30 miles into the tiny town of San Jon, where after a stop for ice and gas we continue west into Tucumcari.

Anyone who traveled Route 66 in its glory days will certainly remember the "Tucumcari Tonight" signs that started popping up along the road back in Texas. Once boasting more than

CHAPTER 6

New Mexico

Uranium Below— Cobalt Above

2,000 motels rooms along its main drag, the sleepy first stop on the way through New Mexico retains all its charms, if fewer rooms.

The Blue Swallow Motel is a certifiable piece of history along this section of Route 66. Run for years by the venerable Lillian Redman, it is now operated by Dale and Hilda Bakke, who have put much effort into preserving the motel's historical features, especially its trademark neon.

Stepping inside one of the Blue Swallow's rooms is like turning back the clock. A huge vintage air conditioner, from the days when the motel proudly offered "100% Refrigerated Air", lines one wall. The bathroom has a window that opens wide, allowing a cooling cross-breeze, and next to each room is an accompanying garage to keep one's car out of the sun on hot days. Then there are the telephones.

The vintage Western Electric models are huge, black and use a dial instead of a keypad. The receivers seem to weigh five pounds each, and although they look like they have been here for years, they are actually new additions to the Blue Swallow. Back in Route 66's heyday, there were no phones in the rooms. The Bakkes purchased them from a restoration house in Chicago and installed them with the help of a grant from U.S. West. (Fear not, laptop luggers: There is an extra jack in the wall for you to connect your modem.)

Between Tucumcari and Albuquerque a succession of failed or failing little towns dot the

Long ago, Tucumcari boasted 2,000 motel rooms. That number has dropped significantly, but there are still plenty of places to stay. The Blue Swallow is a Route 66 classic and is being slowly restored by its new owners.

These days San Jon is little more than a place to jump back on to Interstate 40. But years ago this old mill hummed with workers from the surrounding area.

When Dale and Hilda Bakke decided to install telephones in the rooms, they sought out the real deal. These vintage models were purchased and installed through a grant program offered by a telephone utility.

scrub brush and scattered cattle. On through Montoya, Cuervo, and Santa Rosa, the sky shines in a brilliant blue, a sharp contrast to the ruddy soil beneath.

Jogging north on an older alignment of Route 66, Santa Fe's art colony buzzes with tourists. Galleries dot the streets like Starbucks franchises. Almost everyone here is an artist of some stripe, whether painting or sculpting or crafting new ways to separate tourists from their *dinero*. Keenly aware of its history, the town allows little new construction that does not resemble adobe in some way. Even the downtown parking garage looks like an ancient pueblo.

Weird Science

Driving east on Gibson Avenue, on the southern edge of Albuquerque, you are greeted by a huge billboard welcoming you to "America's Nuclear Weapons Colony." It is an odd contrast, seeing something so many people lived in fear of all their lives so openly embraced, but nuclear weapons and the science surrounding them have always been prone to contradiction. Here, in a top-secret facility inside Kirtland Air Force Base, a cadre of physicists and thin-lipped government types have spent almost 60 years designing the weapons that fueled the Cold War.

At the end of World War II, a small group of researchers, cryptically known as Z Division, set up shop on the site. Four years later, the Sandia Corporation, a subsidiary of Western Electric, took over operations of the facility, and began expanding the labs. As America put its Cold War machine into gear in the 1950s, the facilities grew exponentially, and the lid clamped down activities at Sandia.

Over the years, scientists developed many refinements to both guidance and delivery systems for weapons, and like a true nuclear reaction, their research often fed upon itself, spinning the labs into new areas of study. For example, monitoring test explosions led scientists to develop the Vela satellite, used to detect nuclear tests from space. And Sandia's famed "Z machine," the most powerful X-ray generator in the world, though used primarily to test the effects of a nuclear explosion on different materials, is also able to mimic the temperature on the sun in experiments on black holes. But Sandia's crowning achievements have always been in the business of bombs, and though security remains tight at the labs, across the base there is a public face to the lab's private labors.

The National Atomic Museum elicits an odd combination of pride, shame, and fear. Outside the former ordnance repair shop a collection of missiles and aircraft used to deliver nuclear weapons sit gutted, yet menacing. Inside, though there are thoughtful exhibits on miniature robotics, the life of Marie Curie, and the benefits of nuclear medicine, most of what is on display to the public are tools of mass destruction.

The next-to-last picture show. Even in the age of easily rented home videos, the Odeon Theater in downtown Tucumcari is still the best show in town.

A pair of ship-launched missiles mark the entrance to the National Atomic Museum at Kirtland Air Force Base. A few miles away, the scientists at the Sandia National Laboratories are still designing nuclear weapons.

Most people are familiar with the "Fat Man" and "Little Boy" weapons used in Japan, but the museum holds sundry other devices most of us didn't know existed. There are nuclear mines, meant to be placed in enemy harbors, nuclear shells designed to be fired from conventional artillery, a bazooka-launched warhead, even a backpack-sized bomb designed to be carried into action by a paratrooper (though there is no explanation of how the paratrooper is supposed to get away from the blast after deploying the weapon).

The museum is a testament to both the scientific brilliance and childish naiveté of American officials during the Cold War. They were visionary enough to build a bomb you can carry on your back, but blind to the fact that even using it could trigger a retaliatory firestorm that would destroy the planet. Today, even as the superpowers back away from proliferation, Sandia personnel remain saddled with the dual-mindedness of their predecessors.

In 1998 alone, Sandia delivered more than 20,000 components to the Department of Energy for application in nuclear weapons. Yet at the same time, they were developing safer and more effective ways to monitor existing stockpiles, and dismantle outdated platforms. Accepting cradle-to-grave responsibility for the weapons they design, Sandia scientists have unwittingly provided themselves the ultimate in job security. And as the political face of the world changes, researchers have scurried to meet new challenges.

As individual acts of terrorism become more of a threat than an all-out nuclear war, scientists have developed hand-held electronic "sniffers" that can detect even minute traces of explosives (or illegal drugs) on travelers. They have built virtual reality simulators that allow emergency response teams to train for a nerve gas attack in heavily populated areas. And in the wake of the recent string of high school shootings, researchers are developing sophisticated detection and surveillance systems schools can install to prevent further tragedies.

So in many ways, Sandia is at the forefront of pure research, but remains grounded in the business of death. It is first and foremost a national security laboratory, existing solely to apply scientific and engineering principles to repel foreign or domestic threats. And if by some chance the geopolitical face of the world reverts back to what it once was, Sandia will be ready.

Not far from the National Atomic Museum, hidden deep in the Manzano Mountains, is an underground vault where more than 98 percent of the world's supply of weapons-grade plutonium was once stored. Though it is uncertain how much, if anything, the facility holds today, odds are there is still a good supply of bomb-making supplies somewhere near Sandia. Just in case.

The Old West

West of Albuquerque the old road dips in and out of several Native American reservations, and even from Interstate 40 pueblos are sometimes visible. In the old uranium-mining town of Grants you can get a hearty breakfast with regional options (hash browns or beans, toast or tortilla) before continuing west. Just outside of Thoreau you cross the Continental Divide (rainfall east of it drains into the Atlantic; west of it into the Pacific), and a few miles farther up the road is Gallup, home to the El Rancho Hotel. Over the years it's done double duty, acting both as a home for movie stars shooting westerns in the surrounding desert, and as a location itself. Its rough-hewn log interior has often doubled for an Old West hotel or saloon.

And it is into the Old West for sure. It is unseasonably cold, no more than 40 degrees at first light, but the Arizona border is a few miles away, where the temperature will surely rise. We are in the desert somewhere between Manuelito and the Chief Yellowhorse Trading Post when I spot something by the side of the road up ahead.

At first it looks like a big bag of trash someone had tossed away carelessly, but as we grow closer I notice it's a vibrant purple, not drab green. And by the time I realize it is an elderly woman, she already has her arm out, thumb extended.

It is still freezing, and she wears only a thin coat over her dress. A frail Navajo named Betty, she is trying to get to her son's home on the reservation a few miles across the border. We crank up the heat and give her water as she tells us her story in broken English.

"My husband . . . he's a Mexican up in Gallup," she explains. "Last night he tell me, 'I don't want you anymore—go.'" Though she said she had nowhere to go, he insisted she leave. "'Walk,' he said." And so she did. Gallup is a good 25 miles behind us, and a little quick multiplication tells us she must have been walking all night in the desert cold. We cross into Arizona in an uncomfortable silence, Betty holding her bottle of water and gazing out the back window.

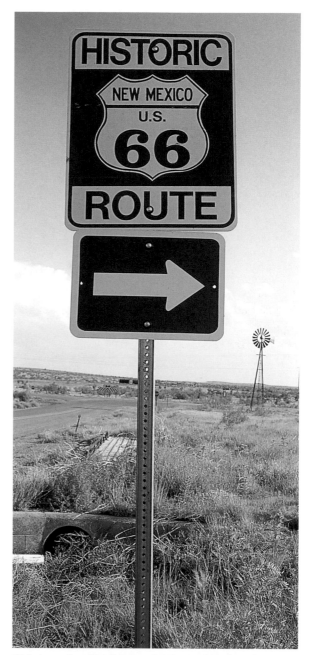

Historic markers like this one dot the roadside from Chicago to Los Angeles. Though you'll still need some good maps to follow it all the way, the familiar brown-and-white signs offer a quick trip back in time for folks who would otherwise stick to the interstates.

Modeled after a similar structure in Paris, the Lorretto Chapel in downtown Santa Fe is one of the many churches and missions that date back to the nineteenth century.

As we approach the exit for Chambers she begins gesturing and saying something about "sonny boy." Though we aren't sure exactly what she means, we figure it be best to exit. She directs us to the nearest gas station and points across a long field to a row of cinder block homes a half-mile away.

"My sonny boy—he live here," she says with a grin. She jumps out of the van and walks across the tarmac of the gas station. I watch in the rearview mirror as she steps down the embankment next to the road and starts across the field.

Gear stowed properly once again, I pulled around and headed back toward the interstate, looking down into the field to see how much of the field she'd crossed. She was gone.

The Beats Go On

When the television series *Route 66* debuted on October 7, 1960, it got a lukewarm reception. Appearing after the second debate between Richard Nixon and John F. Kennedy, it went largely unnoticed, lumped alongside serial westerns and potboiler crime dramas in the public perception. But the weekly travelogue starring Martin Milner and George Maharis was actually on the cutting edge of both technology and popular culture, according to Katie Mills, a cultural critic and researcher from Los Angeles.

"*Playhouse 90* and those sorts of anthology shows that were popular at the time were broadcast live, so there was always this connotation that you were watching theater. *Route 66* was the first show to be shot entirely on location, and made very good use of the emerging technology," she said in a recent interview. In addition, while many television directors were trying to translate the long blocking techniques of theater to the small screen, *Route 66* often used a more cinematic feel, incorporating flashbacks and cinema verité-flavored camera work.

Mills, who received her Ph.D. in Film and Literature from the University of Southern California, also thinks *Route 66* was one of the first regular television shows to give Middle America a realistic portrayal of the Beat Generation, its concerns, and values.

"Beats were treated poorly by the mainstream media at the time, often made fun of. But they were so easy to parody," Mills continued, "They were in the right place at the right time. Just as television was looking for content, the Beats were willing to come on and be kooky. So in some ways it was their own fault.

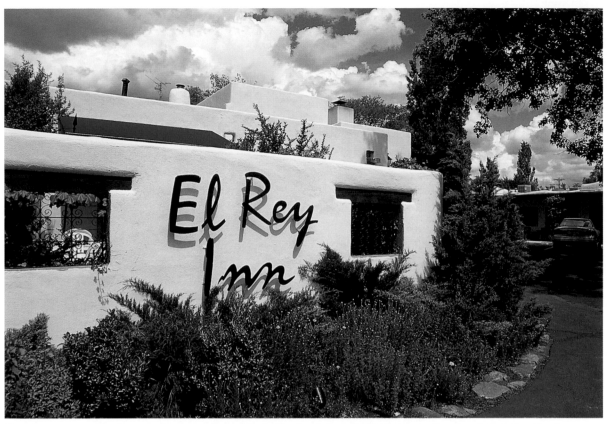

Though rooms near the plaza are often expensive and booked far in advance, the El Rey Inn on the edge of Santa Fe offers luxury accommodations and lush gardens. Its classic adobe exterior is *de rigeur* for buildings new or old.

"Jack Kerouac was on TV a lot in those days, though he personally detested television. He was very shy in general and hated appearing on shows, so he would get drunk first. Then he would go on and be broadcast as this sort of drunken fool. It all became sort of notorious."

While many critics and scholars—Mills included—have long maintained the *Route 66* television series was inspired by *On the Road*, recently published papers show that the book's author also recognized themes in the show. "Kerouac wrote about the similarities in a letter," Mills explained." "He specifically mentioned *Route 66* and how he didn't like it." And if Kerouac liked it little, CBS program executives liked it even less.

"What the show tried to do in its first year, is much different than what it was told to do by CBS in subsequent episodes. Herb Leonard and Sterling Siliphant (the show's producer and main writer) were trying to produce a politically savvy, edgy series," said Mills. "But, and this is very well documented, CBS came back and told them they had to have more 'broads, bosoms, and fun.'"

To be sure, in its early episodes the series was politically charged and dealt with deeper issues than CBS might have cared to visit. Like *The Twilight Zone*, its thinly veiled morality plays often mirrored what was happening in society. The first episode, "Black November," dealt with a wealthy businessman who had murdered two German

69

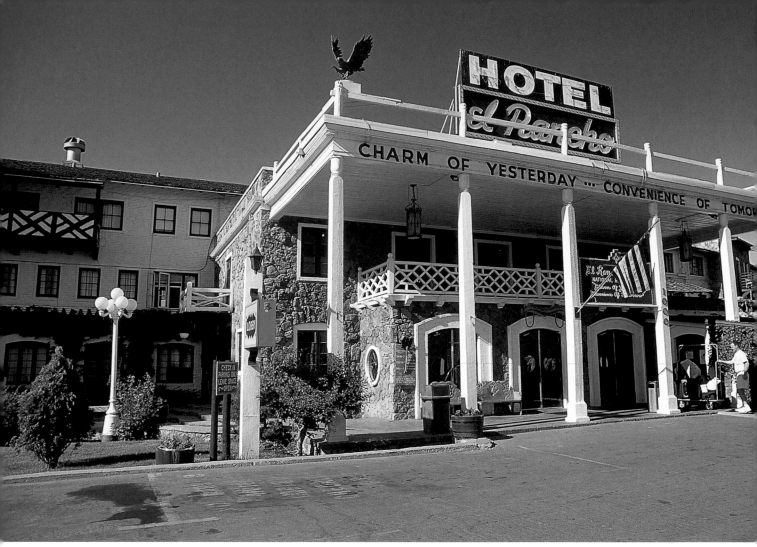

The El Rancho Hotel in Gallup was once a home away from home for actors filming westerns in the nearby countryside. Today it is a required stop for those headed west on Route 66.

POWs as his neighbors watched, after learning his son had been killed in action. In another, Robert Duvall plays a heroin addict trying to kick his habit with the boys' help. Yet another deals with a Native American woman, pregnant after being raped by a white man. But the producers eventually knuckled under to network demands, and it was obvious, according to Mills.

"Leonard and Siliphant were a well respected TV team at that time. They were already producing the show *Naked City*, and a lot of very talented writers, actors and directors worked on *Route 66* before it was over. But you can really see a turnaround where they start introducing lots of guest stars such as Tuesday Weld, Suzanne Pleshette, or Julie Newmar, so there can be more of a romantic plot for these guys." And in addition to the network's insistence on showing a different kind of hip, changes in the show's cast would deal yet another blow to its unique dynamic.

When Maharis was forced to leave the show because of mononucleosis (aggravated by a contract

Over the years many film directors found the El Rancho's rough-hewn interior looked enough like an old West hotel to double as such in their films. While the glory days of the western have long past, TV crews often visit while filming Route 66 documentaries.

dispute say some), Milner teamed up with Glen Corbett, who played Linc, a recently returned Vietnam veteran. For whatever reason, viewers never really bonded with Corbett's character. Perhaps it was because Maharis' departure was too cutely written off in the script to be fully understood, or that no one had ever heard of Vietnam in 1963. Regardless, the show's ratings foundered and it was eventually cancelled.

"It captured the imagination of a lot of people," says Mills. "These guys were young, they didn't have jobs, and they're giving in to this feeling of wanderlust and discovery. I never saw the show as a kid, but knew it was something I wanted to write about."

And though she has written widely about the academic implications of the series, Mills has also driven the real Route 66 end-to-end. Back in 1991, before she was "too busy writing about road trips to actually go on road trips," she drove the old road from Chicago to L.A. "Route 66 is an important part of the postwar road story," she concludes.

In the end, *Route 66* the television series had little to do with Route 66 the road. All but a handful of episodes were filmed far from the old highway itself. But still, the series managed to capture the tinge of wanderlust the road invokes. It beckoned viewers not so much to drive Route 66, as to just drive—not so much to travel, as to explore.

Whoever gave Montana the nickname "Big Sky Country" had obviously never been to Arizona.

Though it is a lighter shade of blue than the deep cobalt of New Mexico, the sky reaches on forever here, until you are certain you can see the curve of the Earth in the distance.

There are little tastes of what the old road was like in every state, but it is here in Arizona where Route 66 remains the purest. There isn't a lot of it, mind you, but what remains is the stuff of dreams. And like any good thing, you must wait for it.

The old highway all but disappears through the first half of Arizona. There are short sections that run for a few miles here and there, but unless you are an amateur archeologist in a four-wheel drive, it is easiest and safest to stick to the interstate for much of the eastern portion of the state. But even on the big road there is plenty to see.

Just off Exit 311 the Painted Desert and Petrified Forest loom north and south of the road, respectively, and an easily driven loop takes you through both parks before depositing you safely back onto Highway 180 at the southern terminus of the preserve. From there it's a quick shot into Holbrook and two unique opportunities for the Route 66 traveler.

The Pow Wow Trading Post deals in all things geological. They stock beautiful turquoise jewelry, legal pieces of petrified wood, and polished stones of every stripe. But in all honesty, they also have a lot of crap. Petrified dinosaur droppings to be precise. I had been looking for that perfect gift to bring back to the wife after this long trip, and after a little deep thought I realized this was not it. Just down the street, however, is something that has drawn travelers without reservations for years.

The Wigwam Motel is a true piece of Americana. There are only two left along the old road, and the one in Holbrook is by far the better for reasons you'll understand better once you get to California. "Have You Slept In A Wig-Wam Lately?" the sign asks. And just down the road from Holbrook sits another Route 66 landmark.

The Jackrabbit Trading Post's trademark yellow signs have lined the roadway since World War II. A simple silhouette of a jackrabbit, with the cryptic "here it is" written alongside, has puzzled travelers for years, and to the sign creator's credit, a good deal of them have stopped in to see exactly what "it" was. Few have been disappointed.

Although the town never made it into Nat King Cole's version of the Bobby Troup song,

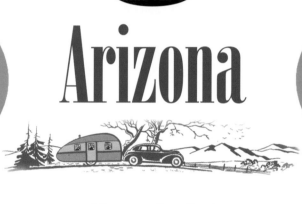

CHAPTER 7

Arizona

Here It Is!

The familiar yellow and black signs for the Jackrabbit Trading Post entice travelers for miles before they actually find out what "it" is.

"(Get Your Kicks on) Route 66," Winslow was immortalized by The Eagles many years later in the Jackson Browne song "Take it Easy." As a testament to the song, town officials have put in a "Standing on the Corner" exhibit downtown, replete with a girl in a flatbed Ford subtly painted onto a window, seemingly reflected from across the street.

There are many small towns along Route 66, but with a population of two, Meteor City ranks as the smallest. Centered around a large geodesic dome, the rough compound is a favorite stop

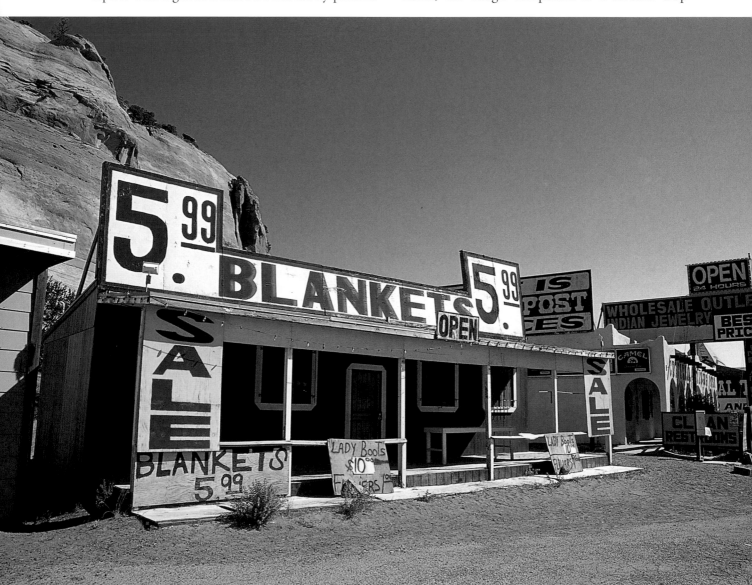

Sitting at the base of dramatic cliffs, the Chief Yellowhorse Trading Post near Lupton is the first stop for gas, cigarettes, and Navajo blankets once you cross the Arizona border.

along this stretch of the old road. You'll find a mixed bag of Route 66 souvenirs, petrified wood, and bric-a-brac related to the hole in the ground just up the road.

Six miles away, more than 20,000 years ago a meteor slammed into the desert floor, leaving a crater almost three miles around. In the late 1800s, a local merchant purchased the land, assuming the crater would yield a rich supply of iron ore. A shaft was dug into the floor of the crater, and the land did indeed produce ore for years. After the mine closed, the crater became increasingly popular as a tourist attraction.

Like many things along Route 66, the Painted Desert in eastern Arizona has to be seen to be believed. From observation points along a long looping drive, you can observe mountains more than 60 miles away with the naked eye.

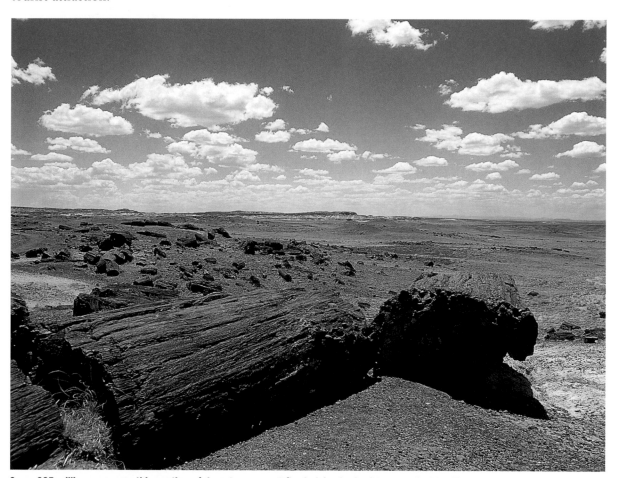

Some 225 million years ago this section of desert was a vast flood plain. As dead trees soaked in silica-laced water, tree tissues crystallized. Today, the Petrified Forest is a perfect compliment to the Painted Desert a few miles north.

Though you can be arrested for removing even a splinter of petrified wood from the national park, a few miles away in Holbrook the Pow Wow Trading Post sells "legal" souvenirs, turquoise, and other Native American artifacts.

It is another one of those things one sees in an encyclopedia as a child, but is in no way prepared for in reality. Stepping out of the visitor center and onto the walkway that rims the crater, perspective takes a powder. Whatever references one uses to gauge the size of things—a person's height or the number of stories in a building—become moot as you peer down into the bottom of the pit.

When the United States entered the space race in earnest, Apollo astronauts trained in the crater, hoping it was a close approximation of the lunar surface. If you look carefully through one of the telescopes mounted on the crater's rim, you can see a plywood cutout of an astronaut holding a U.S. flag at the bottom of the crater.

As you approach the foothills of the San Francisco range, it's easy to see how the line "Don't forget Winona" came to be. The tiny burg just east of Flagstaff is mostly a memory now. Were it not for the fairly new cars parked in front of scattered houses, one could easily assume the place was deserted.

Just up the street in Holbrook, the Wigwam Motel is the last chance for families to stay in an authentic "wigwam." Although there is a similar motel in California, it has gone so far downhill it is not recommended for families.

Climbing into the mountains before Flagstaff, the temperature cools down, and thick pine groves line the roadside. Flagstaff itself is a fine, if unremarkable, city and it's easy to follow the old road through the city center.

We decide to push on into Williams before stopping for the night. It would be one of the best decisions of the trip. The old railroad center is full of history, good food, and cheap lodgings. Even on a weekday evening, the streets are full of people at outdoor cafés, and if there is anyone inside the city limits who is not in a good mood, they do a fine job of hiding it.

The Red Garter Bakery and Breakfast

If ever a town had a love/hate relationship with Route 66, it is Williams. The old logging town 30 miles west of Flagstaff bears the grim distinction of being the last place along the old road to be bypassed. It was here Route 66 officially ceased to be in 1984.

As you step inside the door of the Red Garter the aroma of cinnamon and fresh-brewed coffee wafts over you like a healing wind. Customers sit here and there, reading the newspaper and lingering over coffee, while at a long table near the back, proprietor John Holst chats with overnight guests.

Though gimmick postcards over the years have shown cowboys riding jackrabbits while herding cattle, this larger-than-life statue provides the perfect photo op for connoisseurs of kitsch everywhere.

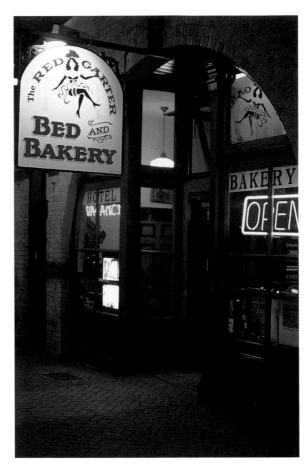

Once a bustling saloon and brothel on the wrong side of Williams, the Red Garter now serves up coffee, pastry, and overnight lodging in the middle of a burgeoning historic district.

When he bought the building more than 20 years ago, it was a run-down warehouse full of used tires and batteries. It had deteriorated to the point that sunshine streamed through gaping holes in the roof. While it is sad to see anything dying from neglect, this particular building's rich and spicy history make it all the more tragic.

"It was built in 1897 by a German immigrant named August Tetzlaff," Holst explains. "He brought all the bricks and building materials in on a flatbed railcar and set it up as a commercial

Proprietor John Holst had been looking for a historic property for years before purchasing what would become the Red Garter. A general contractor before becoming an innkeeper, he gutted and restored the building with loving care.

Another roadside attraction, these oversized arrows often draw the attention of travelers skirting the edges of Twin Arrows, Arizona.

duplex. There was the bordello upstairs that was leased to a madam and a saloon on the first floor that he also leased. Then he put up a little shack out back where he ran his tailor shop."

Tetzlaff's tailor shop faced the town's more respectable business district, while his other enterprise, facing the railroad tracks, did a thriving business as well. The bordello operated under different names right up until the beginning of World War II, according to Holst, although it was a very low-key operation. "They were just called furnished rooms," he says with a grin. In the 1950s the building continued to be used as a rooming house for transients and others down on their luck, before closing and being used for storage.

In 1979 Holst was working as a general contractor rehabbing old buildings throughout northern Arizona and had been looking for a property with potential.

"I kept my eyes open, the same way you might look for a '57 Chevy sitting in someone's backyard. I was looking for a town I could get involved in and own one of these original pieces of history." He eventually found what would become the Red Garter in Williams and began slowly putting it back in shape.

Holst also became active in the community. As an experienced contractor with an eye for historic buildings, he quickly saw the potential Williams had. But in 1984 when it was announced Route 66 would finally be decommissioned, the town's attitude turned sour and many of its residents either left or simply gave up.

"Those were really tough years for us," Holst recalls. "We had to go from this 'grab it while you

You can almost imagine the legion of truck drivers and traveling salesmen that must have had a quick plate of home-cooking at this café in Twin Arrows, before venturing back out onto Route 66.

can, they will never come back' mentality, to physically rebuilding the town and thinking about it in terms of inviting people back. We had to make it a nice enough place that people would be drawn here instead of simply passing through." And while making the downtown area into a historic district was a gargantuan task, changing the town's mindset was even harder.

"It was like pulling teeth," he continues. "A lot of the energetic people moved out, and the whiners and complainers stayed. So what we were left with was a lot of people who were willing to sit back and let others come in and rebuild it." And over the course of a decade, they did just that.

Today, thanks to Holst and many others, Williams is a budding destination community. A vintage rail line takes tourists to the southern rim of the Grand Canyon every morning, a steady stream of Route 66 pilgrims flow through town, and the saloon row that was once the town's shame is a quaint historic district. But the piquant history of the old brothel has not been forgotten.

Lining the wall of the Red Garter are pictures of female guests, draped in red feather boas and winking seductively, or dangling stocking-clad legs from the second-story window while crooking fingers at the camera with a come-hither smile. And though present-day guests revel innocently in the bawdy history of the building, occasionally a ghost from the past reappears. Not long ago an elderly man showed up at the Red Garter and presented its proprietor with a faded red tablecloth.

"He had come in on a freight train years ago, as a hobo," Holst explains. "He paid his two or three dollars for a room for the night, and when he left the next morning he took this cloth that one of the girls used to cover a table, and wrapped his belongings in it when he jumped another train for California. He had kept it all these years and wanted to return it."

Mining Towns

West of Williams, the old road pushes far away from the interstate and up into the desert. Passing south of the Aubrey Cliffs and on through the Hualapai Indian reservation, Route 66 seems stuck in time. There are few cars traveling this stretch, and stepping out onto the hot blacktop it's easy to imagine Okies in broken-down Fords, GIs waiting expectantly with outstretched thumbs and heavy duffels, and long white Cadillacs racing across the desert toward Las Vegas.

A fake squirrel eating a snake atop a plate of burgers is just one sign of Juan Delgadillo's slapstick sense of humor. Visitors are never quite sure what to make of the prankster, who has been pulling gags at the Snow Cap restaurant on Route 66 through thick and thin for decades.

The few towns that remain are little more than wide spots in the road, a few houses and a general store selling cheap beer if even that. Rocky hills shoot up on either side of the road and the sun bakes the ground unmercifully. The last stop before pushing back south toward Kingman is the tiny village of

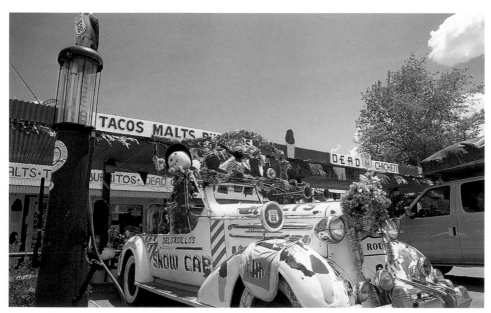

The Snow Cap's company car sits festooned with just about everything outside the landmark attraction in Seligman. Occasionally, Juan starts it up, producing great belches and backfires, just long enough to drive across the street.

81

Inside the Snow Cap, customers jam into the narrow entry to place orders, dodge dime store gags, and enjoy one of the great goofy characters along this stretch of Old Route 66.

Hackberry, site of an old silver mine and home to the infamous Route 66 Visitor Center.

It was run for years by Bob Waldmire, a traveling artist best known for his incredibly detailed "bird's-eye view" map of Route 66. Waldmire's outpost was part archive, part firetrap but still a popular stop for tourists from around the world. One of the road's most colorful characters, Waldmire could often be found driving somewhere along the old road in his "Un-official Route 66 Mobile Information Center"(a bright orange Volkswagen van covered in old highway signs and bumper stickers imploring people to become vegetarian, legalize marijuana, and the old favorite, "Question Authority"). But Waldmire eventually tired of the daily grind and decided to move back to Illinois.

The Route 66 Visitor Center in Hackberry is one of the funky little treasures that dot the Southwest. Cobbled together out of corrugated tin and good intentions, it is under new ownership these days, but remains true to the spirit of its former owner, artist Bob Waldmire.

West of Kingman, Route 66 goes native. None but the brave attempt the primitive road as it winds up into mountain passes and abandoned gold fields. The burned-out hulks of cars at the bottom of passes serve as silent reminders to slow down.

In 1998 he sold the center to John and Kerry Pritchard, a Washington couple who had visited the place and fell in love with it.

While the Pritchards have tidied up some of Waldmire's trademark clutter, the Route 66 Visitor Center retains all of the relaxed charm of its former owner. Though they had planned to renovate the front of the place, people begged them to leave it just as it was.

If the lore of Route 66 seems as rich as a novel at times, perhaps it is because, like a good novel, it reaches its denouement very close to the

In the old mining town of Oatman, burros roam the streets freely. Decades ago, a pack was set free by miners and has been reproducing in the hills ever since. Many shops have signs imploring tourists not to feed them anything but oats, since they tend to metabolize anything else quickly.

end. The slow grade into Oatman is full of hairpin turns and white-knuckle mountain passes. The desert falls away beneath you as you climb through used-up gold fields and abandoned mines. When you finally reach the turnout near Sitgreaves Pass you'll feel inclined to get out and walk around on solid ground, like a sailor returning from an extended voyage at sea.

Just down the side of the mountain a rusted car body lies smashed headlong into the sheer face, the rock above still black from the fire that must have erupted on impact. Below it, a Volvo station wagon, farther still an unrecognizable red ball of steel, and at the very bottom, the back half of a pickup truck lies a few hundred yards from its mangled mate. Near the edge of the cliffs rough-hewn wooden crosses serve as both memorial and warning.

There's still gold in these hills, but what comes out today is a mere trickle compared to the region's glory days. When World War II started, some of the mines were declared nonessential to the war effort, and summarily closed. While many of the miners packed up and left, the few families that stayed have carved a hearty if hard life out of what opportunities remained. But while the human population of Oatman might have dropped, another group has thrived.

Burros were long used by both mines and individual prospectors to carry equipment in and gold out of the hills. When the mines began closing the animals were set free into the mountains, where they have been reproducing ever since. And while the burros roaming the streets of Oatman are descendants of that first generation from the mine, they have grown used to a softer existence.

You smell them before you see them, wandering up and down the narrow main street, licking spilled ice cream from the pavement, begging carrots or oats from obliging tourists and taking cool drinks from children's wading pools. Shopkeepers swat them away from their open doors like a neighbor's errant cat.

Cactus Joe's Cantina in Oatman is built around a huge Saguaro in the center of the room. Inside, a favorite lunch item is the "Stinkin' Garlic Cheeseburger," a patty fried in garlic, topped with garlic and mushrooms, and served with a clove of garlic garnish.

We drop down out of the mountains and cross the Colorado River into California. Luckily, the guardhouse ahead is not turning away refugees. They just want to know if we have any fruit.

Southern California is probably the most photographed real estate on the planet. Since the American film industry sprung up on the edge of Los Angeles in the 1920s, everyone from Laurel and Hardy to *Baywatch* has used the varied terrain as a backdrop. So even if you didn't grow up in California, odds are you spent a good deal of your youth goggling at it on television.

For that reason, by the time you roll into the northern edges of Los Angeles County you have a vague feeling of déjà vu. You recognize the storefronts and skyscrapers and the dull brown haze that hangs over downtown. But before one gets to the palm-lined boulevards of Beverly Hills, or the omnipresent freak show in Venice, you've got to cross the desert.

It is at once alien and familiar. Full of slashing bluffs, dust devils and scrub bushes, the Mojave is neither the pure sand desert you expect nor the Martian landscape it so often approximated in 1950s science fiction movies. But it is hard land all the same, and if it feels this brutal in an air-conditioned van, then crossing it in a Model T or Conestoga is unimaginable.

CHAPTER 8

California

The Garden of Eden

On the west edge of Needles, you rejoin I-40 for a spell, before exiting and rejoining the old road. Route 66 arcs north through the old town of Goffs before curving south again toward Amboy. And as you pass under the interstate, a railroad track runs high on an embankment on your right. Against its side fellow travelers have left their mark.

Spelled out in stones laid carefully into the steep grade, the messages are simple: a name or two, perhaps just initials. The most ornate (obviously done in the cool of the morning) have names and dates and offer universal slogans such as "Cruisin'!" and "Gettin' our kicks." Most are legible, although a few have lost their hold in the sandy soil.

The old road continues on through Essex, Chambless, and Amboy, making a long dip south skirting the rims of dried-out lakebeds. Though the remains of the town of Bagdad are on this stretch between Amboy and Ludlow, the movie *Bagdad Café*, which sparked much German interest in the old road, was actually shot a few miles farther on, in Newberry Springs.

As you drive south and west out of Barstow, you pass through the last of the Mojave and the last section of open road on Route 66. Soon it will be into the urban sprawl of Los Angeles, where the old highway traverses barrios and bedroom communities. But before the journey draws to a close, there's one last bit of history, just outside of Helendale.

Once a kitschy stop along Route 66, the Wigwam Motel near Rialto had deteriorated into a dive used mostly by the prostitutes working the street in front.

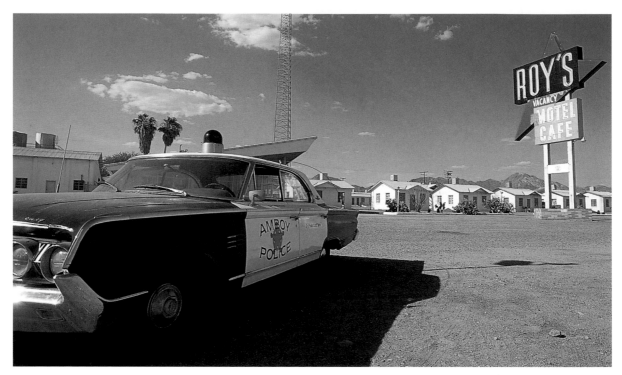

A vintage police car sits parked outside Roy's Motel and Café in Amboy, California. The Mojave landmark has long been a stop-off for travelers and servicemen from the nearby Marine Corps training facilities, and often shows up in print ads and television commercials.

Exotic World Burlesque Museum

Down a bumpy road on the edge of town, a set of tall white columns marks the entrance to the Exotic World Burlesque Museum, home of the "Movers and Shakers." As we follow the sandy lane down into a compound of outbuildings and trailers, former stripper Dixie Evans is taking it off. She's taking it all off.

"You *would* show up when I'm scrubbing out my microwave," she says, deftly removing a pair of rubber gloves and pulling up a chair at a shaded table outside the museum.

At 75, Evans is, in the finest sense of the words, a classy broad. She moves gracefully, quoting Aristophanes as easily as Groucho Marx, pointing out displays and hitching up her pants with an air of self-assuredness no mere 70-year-old could muster.

She was born Mary Lee Evans in Long Beach in 1926. He father died when she was a child, leaving Mary Lee and her mother alone. She set out to become a dancer, hoping to land a slot in a chorus line. And though those goals proved elusive, Evans finally got work as a page in a musical review.

"Oh it was easy enough work," Evans recounts. "You had a cute little costume and every once in a while you walked out with a card listing the next act or pulled back the curtains as the shows began." Evans went on the road with the show, but it went broke a few weeks later, and she found herself stranded in San Francisco.

"Well, one of the girls mentioned there was a strip place up the street," she recalls with a raucous laugh. Evans signed on to work at the club, where she found great friendship and support from her fellow dancers and launched a new career. "It was the beginning of a whole new beautiful world for me."

In Evans' heyday, many of the performers were billed as look-alikes of famous actresses. "We had the Loretta Young of burlesque, the Lauren Bacall of burlesque, the Sophia Loren of burlesque," Evans recalls. "I was the Marilyn Monroe of burlesque."

Indeed she was. The fading black-and-white publicity photo on a museum wall shows Evans in a beaded dress and heavily made-up, younger but just as blond, posing as Marilyn. The resemblance is uncanny.

Unlike the gentlemen's clubs and porn houses of today, the burlesque theaters in which Evans worked attracted both men and women. While never considered high art, the risqué skits were often biting social satire, skewering figures out of the day's headlines. One of those figures was Joe DiMaggio, who had recently divorced Hollywood's hottest starlet. And while a true statistical analysis might tell a different story, even a fleeting belief in fate leads you to believe that sooner or later "the Marilyn Monroe of burlesque" would collide with the real-life Joe DiMaggio. Eventually, she did: in Florida.

Evans was doing her Monroe act in a Miami Beach nightclub when the manager came to her table and told her DiMaggio was there and wanted to meet her. She told him it would be rude to leave the person with whom she was sitting, and Mr. DiMaggio would have to come back another time. But after some prodding from both her friend and the manager, she finally agreed to sit with Joltin' Joe.

"He was sitting at a table with Grantland Rice, the sportswriter, and Skinny D'Amato, who ran the 500 Club in Atlantic City," Evans recalls. "They were sitting around cracking jokes and such."

She enjoyed a drink and a few laughs with DiMaggio and his friends, but became increasingly uneasy about performing her Monroe impersonation with him there. The couple had just divorced, and Evans' routine made great sport of DiMaggio.

Though the old town of Bagdad is little more than a memory today, the Bagdad Café in Newberry Springs was the inspiration for both a movie and short-lived television sitcom. The story of a Bavarian woman who leaves her husband and stays to work at the restaurant is extremely popular throughout Europe.

"He said, 'Go ahead, I don't mind,' but I was still just shaking in my boots," she says. But ever the trouper, she mustered up her nerve and went on. Standing up and backing away from the breezeway table, Evans lights up as she goes into the act she performed so long ago.

Oh Boo hoo hoo…why shouldn't I cry?
Joe, you walked out and left me flat.
You didn't want me anymore: you left no doubt
of that. So now you're gone and I'm all alone,
Thank heavens you left your bat!

Evans grabbed DiMaggio by the tie and dragged him into the spotlight with her as she continued the sex-kitten routine. "He had to be halfway embarrassed, being pulled out there in the spotlight with me like that," Evans laughs. But ever the gentleman, DiMaggio took it all in fun.

Evans' friend, Jenny Lee, originally started Exotic World. Also a former burlesque dancer, Lee

Dixie Evans, once billed as "The Marilyn Monroe of Burlesque," runs the Exotic World Burlesque Museum on an old goat farm outside of Helendale. Once a year she sponsors a Miss Exotic World Pageant, reuniting performers from the golden days of burlesque.

Though there are still plenty of girls out there willing to take their clothes off on stage, and a flourishing gentleman's club circuit to employ them, Evans thinks they bear little resemblance to the glory days of burlesque. "You can't compare Grandma's old iron skillet to a microwave," she laughs.

The End of the Road

South of Victorville and on through San Bernardino, there are few unspoiled pieces left of the original road, and any enjoyment you get from finding them is balanced by all the backtracking through city streets one does to get there. And descending down out of the mountains and into the Inland Empire region of suburban L.A., there is a tinge of regret that the journey is almost over.

Route 66 becomes Foothill Boulevard here, passing through Rialto, Rancho Cucamonga, and Upland. The Wigwam Motel sits just north of the road on the edge of Rialto, mirroring the Wigwam Village back in Arizona, but its southern California cousin has seen better days. The pool is cracked and empty, and the desk attendant waits in a darkened room behind bulletproof glass. Once a stop for families on their way to Disneyland, the motel's only customers these days are prostitutes and the people who employ them.

From here on, Route 66 is a confusing hodgepodge of different possibilities. A left turn could take you down the route from the 1930s, while turning right might mean a trip down the 1950s alignment. And while there are still historic points along the way, it is all city driving, maddeningly slow and mostly uninteresting. Soon the glory and history of what was Route 66 becomes the glitz and smog and noise of Los Angeles.

The Mayor of the Mother Road

Almost before they had pulled up the last markers on the old road, there were already groups plotting to save Route 66. While there have been government dollars put into play here and there,

owned several nightclubs and had become quite successful off the stage before being stricken with cancer. Lee sold her clubs, and moved to the desert for the less stressful lifestyle. Evans visited often, and eventually stayed on to care for Lee and the fledgling museum. Although Lee passed away a short time later, Evans has kept her dream alive and growing. No small feat, since entry to the museum is free.

"I don't know where the money comes from, but we just keep going," Evans explains. While Exotic World contains many rare items—Sally Rand's fans, a beaded dress of Marilyn Monroe's, and Jayne Mansfield's heart-shaped divan—Evans would like to expand it even more, turning it into a Hall of Fame for performers from all over the world.

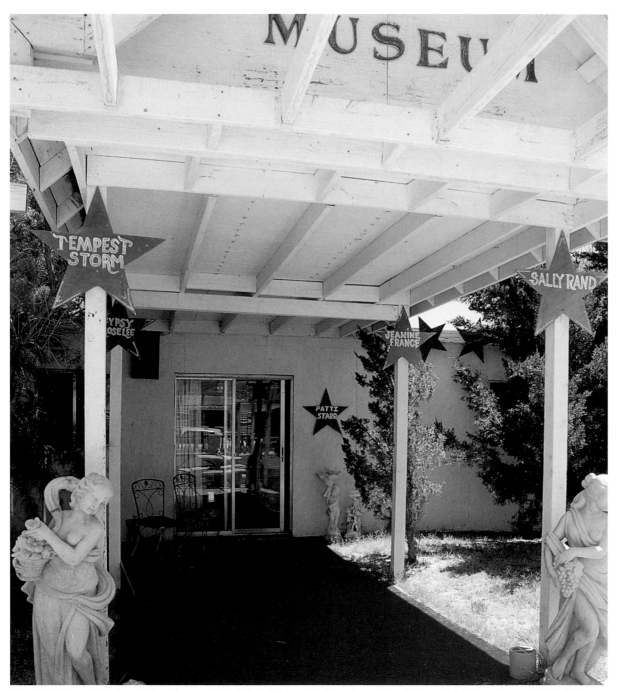

When Dixie Evans' friend and fellow dancer Jenny Lee was diagnosed with cancer, she sold her nightclubs and moved to the high desert for the relaxed lifestyle. As her health failed, Evans moved in to help care for her, and took over the operation and expansion of what became Exotic World.

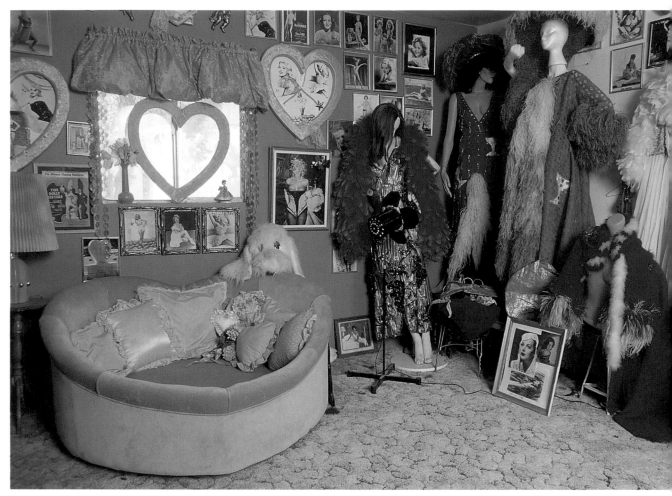

Jayne Mansfield's heart-shaped divan is one of many rare exhibits housed at Exotic World. Performers and collectors alike often donate items to the museum, believing they will be in their rightful home.

the effort to resurrect 66 is mostly the work of regular folks. State by state, mile by mile, they've slapped on a coat of paint here, held a fundraiser there, and coaxed a few dollars out of the county highway departments everywhere. Like a good old-fashioned barn raising, Route 66 is being put back together a mile at a time by its neighbors. And if Route 66 is indeed the "long, thin town" songwriter Kevin Welch describes, then its mayor is undoubtedly Angel Delgadillo.

Delgadillo, a soft-spoken barber from Seligman, Arizona, was born on a dirt road that would become 66 in 1927. One of nine children, he attended school in Seligman before venturing off to the Pacific Barber College in Pasadena, California, also on Route 66. After graduation, he got an apprenticeship at a small barbershop in Williams, Arizona, also on Route 66. When it came time to venture out on his own, Delgadillo returned to Seligman and starting cutting hair in a one-chair

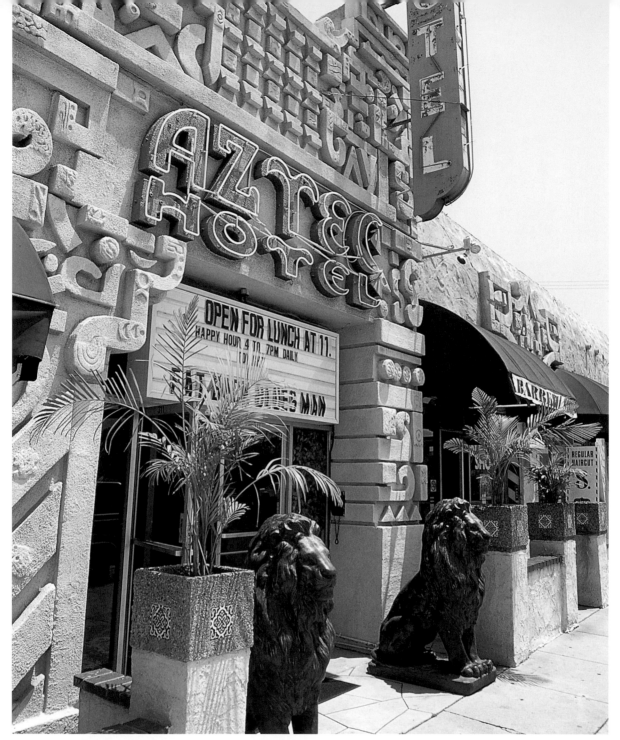

Designed by Robert Stacy-Judd in the 1920s, the Aztec Hotel in Monrovia is on the National Register of Historic Deeds. Judd designed several other area buildings, including the Masonic Temple in Tujunga, First Baptist Church of Ventura, and the Atwater Bungalows in Elysian Park.

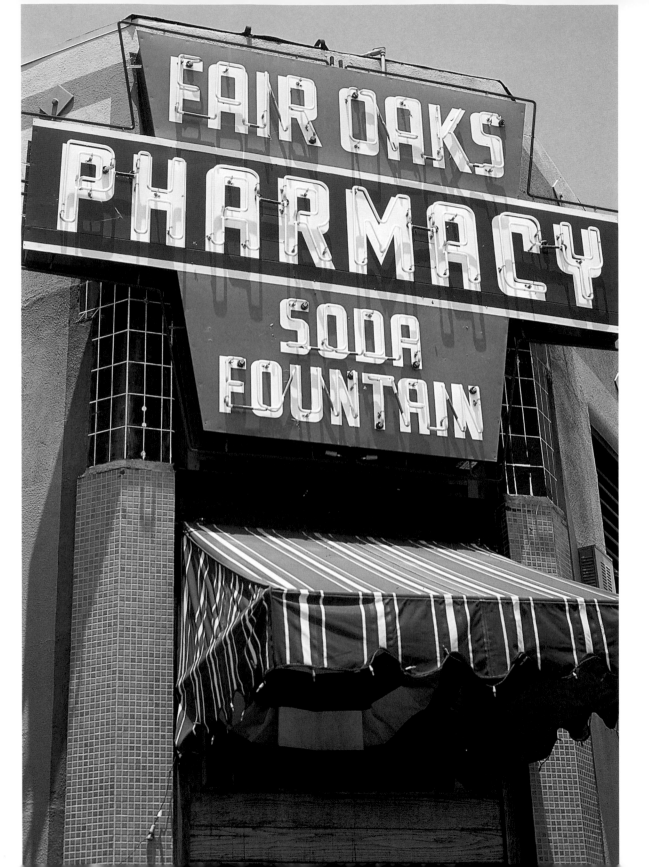

shop on Main Street—also Route 66—where he's been ever since.

Having spent his entire life along this stretch of Old Route 66, one can only guess at the heartache Delgadillo must have felt as he stepped out of his shop and looked at Main Street on September 22, 1978, the day traffic was officially redirected off Route 66 and onto I-40 to the south.

"All through that last summer you had to run just to get across the street. The traffic was so heavy: 9,000 cars every day," Delgadillo explains. "Then, it was gone. You could lay down and go to sleep in the middle of Main Street if you wanted. It was completely dead."

Delgadillo knew the historic role Route 66 had played not only in Seligman's past, but the nation's. And while many people in the towns along this old stretch were preparing for the worst, Delgadillo refused to join them. Instead, he became an evangelist, gently prodding people to band together and lobby state officials to grant the road historic status.

"They thought we were nuts," he says, beaming. "But we had to do something, and stick together. That's why we formed the Historic Route 66 Association of Arizona. Now there are groups in every state and all over the world." Delgadillo, though simply trying to save the town to which he had devoted his life, started a movement that spread up and down the length of Route 66 and around the globe.

For that reason and many more, Delgadillo has become a beacon for Route 66 travelers. Every day, people pull into Seligman wanting to meet the man they read about in a book or saw in a video or interviewed on television. And if by chance Angel isn't there, another member of the Delgadillo fam-ily is there to greet them. Just down the street from the barbershop, Angel's older brother Juan runs the Snow Cap. Part drive-in, part vaudeville routine, the wildly decorated restaurant is impossible to miss as you roll into town.

Juan is fond of jokes. Nothing sophisticated, mind you: dime store gags, melted forks, or wads of dirty napkins will do just fine. He uses them all to great effect on the stream of Route 66 travelers passing through.

Pity the poor European tourist who finally gets his order out in broken English, only to get fake mustard squirted at his wife, his change given to someone else. And the menu is as comic as the Snow Cap's proprietor, offering "Cheeseburgers (with Cheese), Hamburgers (no ham)," and the ever-popular entree, proudly displayed in large letters on a sign out front, "Dead Chicken."

There are thousands of images that depict Route 66 as it once was. The stark black-and-white images taken during the Depression by Dorothea Lange, the dusty prose of Steinbeck, and the wise-cracking blues of Woody Guthrie all contribute in a way. Yet, if there is a definitive picture of all this old road once was, and continues to be, it is Main Street Seligman on a Tuesday afternoon.

The street is mostly quiet, save for a trickle of Route 66 travelers coming mostly from the east. At the Snow Cap, pennants flap in the breeze, buoyed by the smell of grilling burgers. Just up the street, Angel Delgadillo neatly folds his apron and lays it on the barber chair his father bought in 1929.

"I started telling people about six months before I was going to retire: 'You're going to have to find another barber,'" he recalls. "I'm still going to be coming in here every day, and you might see me cutting hair once in a while, but it's all public relations work." And true to his word, he often

On Mission Street in Pasadena, the Fair Oaks Pharmacy serves up old-fashioned sundaes and ice cream sodas from behind their vintage counter. In addition to its retro soda fountain, Fair Oaks is still a working drugstore filling as many prescriptions as egg creams.

The Mayor of the Mother Road. Angel Delgadillo, a gentle barber from Seligman, Arizona, founded the first Historic Route 66 Association and is responsible for much of the preservation work that followed. People from around the world travel to Seligman to visit his shop and meet him in person.

The ferris wheel on Santa Monica Pier is one of many carnival rides that attract tourists and locals alike. Like Roy's back in Amboy, the pier is a favorite location for both amateur and commercial photographers.

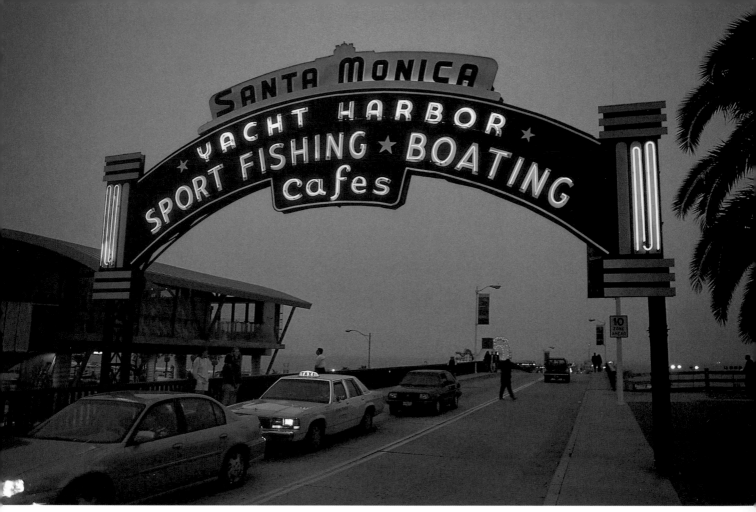

Though Route 66 technically ended a few blocks away, the Santa Monica Pier has become a symbolic last stop for a generation of Route 66 pilgrims. As night falls over the Pacific, a stream of traffic departs, leaving only the hardcore fisherman and barflies behind.

obliges visiting tourists, writers, and photographers with a haircut or shave.

The souvenir shop next door connects to his shop, and every few minutes someone will poke their head in, ask if they can have his autograph or take a picture. He refuses no one. He has grown to expect the pilgrims, and though he is never sure just how many will arrive on a certain day, he knows they will always come.

Delgadillo's life story and the history of Route 66 are intertwined, almost to the point of being one. Sadly, more of his life is behind him now than ahead, and when people reach that

point that they often reflect on what was, and what could have been. As a barber, he could have worked anywhere in the world, but instead returned to his hometown. When he retired, he was cutting the hair of the grandchildren of his first customers. And the smile on his face as he relates that fact leads one to believe he is comfortable, if not proud, of the choices he made as a young man.

The rebirth of interest in Route 66 would not have happened without Angel Delgadillo. The Route 66 community, the town of Seligman, and the world will be a poorer place without him.

Epilogue

There is a damp chill on the Santa Monica Pier. The maze and haze of Pasadena, Los Angeles, and Beverly Hills (where, incidentally, we saw neither swimming pools nor movie stars) are long behind us, as are the thousands of miles of the United States we traveled.

Seagulls squawk above, diving occasionally after a fisherman's bait while music from the ferris wheel booms loudly in the distance. As the sun begins to set over the Pacific, we both sit silently, reflecting on the trip.

There are hundreds of things that come to mind: the face of the tree-trimmer in Amarillo who turned out to be an incredibly talented stencil artist, a couple in Oklahoma having a plate of barbecue and the way the man caressed the back of his wife's hand as he slid her a toothpick, and the look on the face of a little boy in a Mojave diner, whom we had just bought a soda, as his father took it away from him and drank it himself.

We've done our best to give you a flavor of what Route 66 is like today and what it might have been like in the past. Though it is a sad admission for a writer to make, words alone can't do justice to the power held in that old, crumbling pavement.

If you ever have the chance to drive it, as an athletic shoe company might say: Just do it. Take along some good maps, but don't concern yourself with staying on the exact alignment from 1926, 1936, or 1956. Pick your way along as best you can. If the road looks good, take it. If you are unsure, turn around and go back. And if by chance you're traveling with a photographer who has a brand new compass he is itching to use, throw that sucker out the window first chance you get.

Thanks for coming along.

Gas Station
Memories

Dedication

Gas Station Memories is dedicated to all the unknown petroleum company staff photographers, documentary image makers, and hired shooters who never quite received their fair share of accolades. With work stored in photographic archives and company historical files, these visionary camera men and women continue to illuminate the past as recorders of streetside history. Through their discerning eyes–and by means of the silver-halide crystal–modern historians may glimpse highlights of yesterday's classic gas stations. For all those who cherish the early years of the American filling station and the golden age of the automobile, these pictures are worth a thousand words.

ACKNOWLEDGMENTS

Many thanks to the organizations that assisted. A wipe-the-windows smile to The American Petroleum Institute; Atlantic Richfield; Bennett Pump Co.; Chevron Corp.; Circa Research & Reference; the Don Garlits Museum; Gilbarco, Inc.; Michael Garman Productions; Mobil Oil Corp.; Phillips Petroleum Co.; The PoweRoyal Co.; Shell Oil Co.; Texaco Inc.; Tokheim Corp.; and the University of Louisville Ekstrom Library.

Additional thanks to all those specialists working under the hood, including Judy Ashelin; Bill Carner; Douglas Elmets; Robert Finney; Mark Frutchey; Kathy Holland; Joan Johnson; Mary Keane; David LeBeau; Dottie McKenna; Marsha Meyer; Rita Simon; Thomas Thompson; and Cherie Voris.

An attendant's salute to Tom Allen; Warren Anderson; Kent Bash; Scott Benjamin; Billie and Bob Butler; Pat Chappell; C. J. Conner; Jim and Mary Edds; Wayne Henderson; Jerry Keyser; Marty Lineen, Jr.; Frank J. Liska; Ed Love; Jeff Pedersen; Steve Perrault; Hal Polsen; Andrea and David Priebe; Howard B. Ramsay; Gary Rawlings; Steve Smith; Peter Tytla; and Walter Webber.

Special high-octane thanks to Gyvel Young-Witzel for her assistance; Clare Patterson's Red Horse Museum; and Robert McCalla and staff at the White Eagle Mall. Before the tank is full, I straighten my bowtie for Motorbooks editor Michael Dregni, for suggesting this publication and guiding it to the pumps.

INTRODUCTION

In America, gasoline stations are the type of businesses that exist mostly in the fringes of our recollection.

We love our automobiles and think nothing of carrying on talking for hours and hours about the drive we took to the top of Pikes Peak or the kicks we got on Route 66. Convertibles, steel-belted radials, fuel-injection, and the latest advancements in speed and comfort are all appropriate topics of discussion.

Yet when the point of conversation turns to refueling stations, the majority of modern-day motorists clam up. Recent controversies over environmental accidents have cast petroleum refiners in an unfavorable light. News reports exposing the inaccurate measuring practices of a few dishonest operators have compounded the image problem. To make matters worse, federal programs funded by fuel levies continue to promise higher prices at the pumps.

It's no wonder that America's unromantic refueling stations have been taken for granted. They have been a purely utilitarian necessity. But today, as the global transmutation of trade, government, and custom threatens to homogenize the world, a nation of unique individuals pines away for the "good old days." Cultural institutions with truly American roots are viewed with nostalgia. As advancing technology forces the recollections of yesteryear out from the shadows, the golden history of the gas station is being rediscovered.

Today, the naive icons of an innocent age are perceived with new vision. The specter of planetary oil depletion and the phasing out of the internal-combustion engine hover before us in the near future. Suddenly the gas station signs, gasoline dispensers, advertising images, maps, toys, and a multitude of other items once foolishly disregarded are now treasured keepsakes.

MELLOWED 80 MILLION YEARS

While brutes were hatched from eggs in OKLAHOMA

Deep in Oklahoma lie the producing sands of the Cambrian and Ordovician Ages—in some places more than a mile below the surface. Out of them comes the rich Cambro-Ordovician crude oil which is refined and blended into Sinclair Opaline Motor Oil—crude oil which had already mellowed for millions of years when dinosaurs lumbered their clumsy way above its hidden reservoirs.

Being the oldest of the Mid-continent crude oils, Cambro-Ordovician crude has had the full benefit of Nature's age-long mellowing and filtering process. Together with the other

crudes with which it is blended, it averages more than 80 million years of Nature's priceless treatment.

In process of manufacture into Sinclair Opaline Motor Oil, these crudes are not only de-waxed—they are also freed from non-lubricating petroleum jelly, a process which requires chilling the oil down to as low as 60° F. below zero.

Have the nearest Sinclair dealer change your oil to Sinclair Opaline according to the Sinclair Law of Lubrication Index. You'll find that with Opaline in your crankcase you'll use

up less oil in the heat of fast driving. This is not only a direct economy; it is also an indication that there is less friction on your bearings. Engineers know that the oils which last longest lubricate best.

NOTE: *For those who prefer a Pennsylvania grade motor oil, Sinclair dealers also sell Sinclair Pennsylvania Motor Oil made 100% from the costliest Pennsylvania grade crude (mellowed a hundred million years) and de-waxed and freed from petroleum jelly at as low as 60° F. below zero. Sinclair Refining Company (Inc.), New York, N.Y.*

Tune in Monday evenings 30 NBC Stations   SINCLAIR MINSTRELS

Copyrighted 1932 by Sinclair Refining Company (Inc.)

SINCLAIR OPALINE

MOTOR OIL   REG. U.S. PAT. OFF.

From the oldest Mid-continent crudes

Service You Will Remember

The history of the American gas station is rich with the symbols of service, speed, power, and value. Back in the "good old days," the friendly service station attendant was always ready to wipe the windows and check the oil. Friendly service was always the kind "you will remember," and products bristled with pride and claims of superiority above all others. At the same time, potent meanings were represented by the use of powerful brand names. With this unending proliferation of exciting imagery and fantastic claims, how could Americans not fall completely in love with the automobile, and more importantly, the roadside Service Station? *Michael Witzel © 1993*

In an all out effort to capture the highlights from this unpretentious past, time fragments from a bygone age are being collected, catalogued, and archived for future reference.

Our great car culture, born almost a century ago, and the gasoline stations that

Mellowed 80 Million Years Dinos

According to the organic theory, petroleum was formed during prehistoric times when vast oceans covered much of the earth's surface. As tiny plants and animals that thrived along the coastlines died, their remains eventually settled to the bottom where a variety of bacteria caused them to decay. Sedimentary particles of fine sand and mud eventually covered the plant and animal remains and formed into hard beds of rock. As layer upon layer of stone compacted the remains, the combining forces of bacteria, pressure, heat, and other natural forces caused the materials to be transformed into oil and natural gas. As time progressed, tiny droplets of oil and minute amounts of gas moved from their original mud beds into other forms of porous rock, such as sandstone or limestone. Sinclair played on this theory during the 1930s with a series of advertisements featuring dinosaurs, touting this "age-old mellowing and filtering process" provided by mother nature and the passage of time. *Courtesy Atlantic Richfield Company*

The art of being human

FROM a woman motorist comes one of our most cherished bouquets.

"Last Saturday," she writes, "I was driving through open country and a tire blew out. It was miles to the nearest garage. There was no place I could go for help.

"Cars came by—several of them. But not one stopped—until one of your big tank trucks came along. Before I so much as raised a finger, the driver saw my predicament, jumped down, and offered to help.

"In just a few minutes, he had changed the tire—and had driven off followed by my gratitude. I call that a pretty courteous and neighborly gesture for an employee of a big and busy company!"

We value this letter because, like many of its kind, it is proof that an old-established policy of this company has born fruit. That policy is this . . . courtesy to patrons is as vital as quality of product.

The five thousand men who drive Gulf tank trucks are schooled to observe certain rules of the road which are nothing more or less than common courtesy. If you drive toward a Gulf tank truck, the driver will give you all the road the truck allows. If you approach one from behind, you'll be given ample room to pass—quickly, before you wear out your horn or your temper. And if you break down on the road, there is a chance that your first offer of help will come from the driver of a Gulf tank truck.

Gulf is proud to have grown big. But it is even prouder of staying human.

GULF REFINING COMPANY

powered its growth have evolved into an entity more extensive than early tinkers could ever have imagined.

In itself, our mobile society cannot easily be measured or analyzed. The motorcar and its influence has so guided the development of this nation that to examine its impact from a neutral vantage point would be impossible.

Maybe someday, when all of the businesses that now sell refined petroleum have been refitted for electric battery recharge, sale of hydrogen, or some other miracle fuel of the future, we will be able to step back and view to what extent the automobile and its gasoline-pumping companion has affected human existence.

By then, the paper of this book will have become old and brittle, the pictures printed within faded and even more unfamiliar. The new commuters of tomorrow's roadways, whatever their manner of conveyance, will eagerly browse through these images of antiquity to dream, imagine, and maybe even wonder...whatever became of those great gas stations?

Super Shell Wayne 60
Artist C.J. Conner captured art imitating life with this painting of a Wayne pump unit used as a temporary home for a pair of birds. As more and more vintage dispensing units and gas stations are retired from use, only photographs and images like these will remain to remind us of the way things were. *C.J. Conner © 1993*

Previous page
Gulf's Art of Being Human
Back in the days when physicians still visited patients in their homes, it wasn't at all unusual for Gulf's company truck drivers to assist motorists stranded along the roadways. According to advertisements of the period, drivers of Gulf tanker trucks could be counted on for courteous driving as well as spur of the moment assistance. Like their friendly counterparts at the neighborhood service station, they were eager to please and would perform any duty toward this end. Helping the hapless automobile owner without charge was the type of advertising money could not buy. For the Gulf Oil Company, this friendly service attitude was more than just a great public relations vehicle; it was an important part of "the art of being human." *Photograph provided, and reprinted with permission, by Chevron Corporation and its subsidiary, Chevron U.S.A. Inc.*

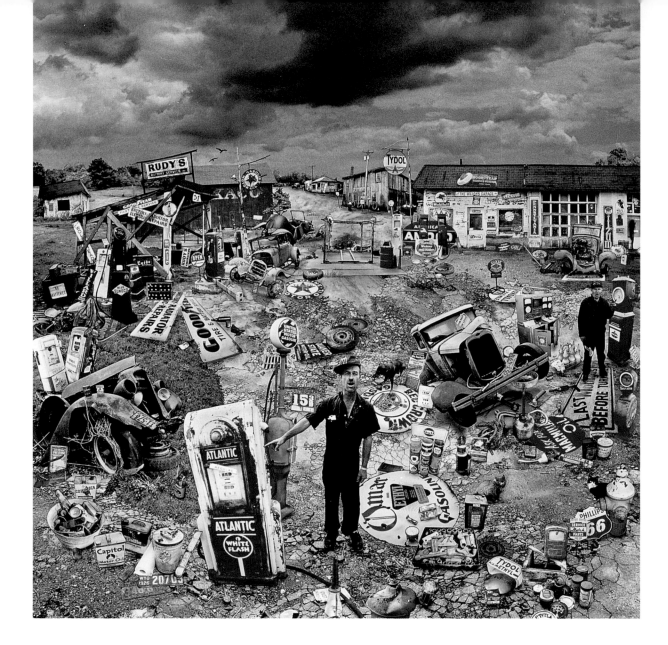

All Sold Out

Artist Peter Tytla's handmade collages are usually made up of over 200 individual photographs. His favorite place to hang out is the salvage yard, a fertile breeding ground for many of his most useful collage components. Five weeks of meticulous labor goes into each one of his humorous scenes, with each individual photograph carefully cut out, re-touched, and glued into place. As all the elements slowly come together, Tytla "begins to cook," carefully placing every photographic fragment in its proper place, as if by intuition. The resulting photographic composite becomes a frenetic jumble of automotive parts, gasoline station artifacts, and eclectic junkyard scenery. In the midst of the visual cacophony, an outspoken individual usually takes center stage. For petroliana aficionados and those bent towards the appreciation of the American road (and the junkyards that often adjoin them), Tytla's collages are truly an amazing sight to behold. (Original art 30inx40in). *Peter Tytla © 1993*

Chapter 1

STATIONS

When Laessig and Grenner formed the Automobile Gasoline Company in St. Louis, no one had to explain to the pair what was wrong with refueling an automobile. By 1905, most Missouri vehicle owners knew that powering a motorcar with gasoline was inconvenient, messy, and extremely dangerous.

So, in an effort to enhance the onerous procedure, the partnership decided to simplify it. By attaching a flexible section of hollow rubber tubing to an upright storage tank, they pumped life into a roadside ritual in dire need of improvement. The filler hose became the new standard for refueling.

Two years later, Standard Oil of California duplicated the effort by installing the first filling station of its kind on the West Coast. Incorporating the flexible hose as an important part of the operation, area sales manager John McLean inaugurated the flagship station for the new Seattle territory.

As filling a gas tank became more practical, former skeptics began to endorse the automobile. By the mid-1920s, improved roads cut a bold path across America–shifting the nation's cultural center of gravity away from the cities. By then, over 250,000 stations were pumping gas along the way.

Wippel's Gas Station, Ellensburg, Washington
About twenty years ago, every small town in America had a gasoline station like Wippel's. Today, those types of businesses are all closed, supplanted by some form of gasoline convenience store. The act of grabbing a bag of potato chips and a soft-drink (in a "Jurassic Park" commemorative cup) at the neighborhood quick-shop is a perfectly normal activity for children growing up in the modern age. The idea of yesterday's general store has been resurrected— albeit reshaped and re-formatted for a brave new world. Now, it serves an expanded roster of functions far superior to its predecessor: local teenage hangout, smoke-shop, center for individual video gaming, snack-center, touch-tone communications hub, beer and wine stockade, and a reliable place for the boys in blue to get their fresh coffee and doughnuts. Aren't the changes that progress brings a wonderful thing?

With the sale of oil and motor fuel now an established industry, refiners began to revamp their sales outlets. The disheveled image of the tumble-down gasoline shack became an economic liability. Slowly, America's unorganized rabble of refueling outposts evolved into a network of serious service stations.

Now, stately structures with all the respectability of the local bank and library were constructed along the roadsides. Polished stone and terra-cotta soon adorned service station buildings worthy of any civic office. Neo-classical architecture became the rage as many gas stations cleaned up their image.

A few bold operators experimented with more outlandish styles as filling stations assumed the shape of lighthouses, seashells, castles, windmills, and even giant gasoline pumps. To the delight of many, the Pure Oil Company constructed stations replicating small English cottages. Oil canisters replaced pies cooling on the windowsill.

As the gasoline station searched for its identity, the great depression of '29 sent prices tumbling. In some cities, the average price per gallon dropped to ten cents! 2.5 million vehicles came to a grinding halt. To bolster sagging revenues, the practice of selling tires, batteries, and accessories sud-

Early Curbside Pump, circa 1915
By 1915, virtually any business owner who wished to sell gasoline could have a pump and storage tank installed outside their shop and advertise gasoline. Because thousands of these new income-generating outlets could be easily obtained by the oil concerns in a matter of months, the need to secure new real estate was bypassed. Profits from the sale of gas could be realized in a very short time. Refiners had only to install pumps, deliver the gas, and collect their huge share of the profits. Individual shop owners would handle sales and collect the generous revenues. Within a very short amount of time, the curbside gasoline pump (such as this Tokheim Curb Post Outfit No. 14) could be seen from almost any streetside vantage point. *Courtesy Tokheim Corporation*

Moran Gas Tank Wood Dipstick
Before the widespread use of remote gasoline gauges, today's simple glance at the dashboard to check fuel level was not possible. Early station attendants and do-it-yourself motorists usually had to check their gasoline receptacle manually. For the most part, that meant inspecting the tank for fluid level and listening for the tell-tale sounds of "being full" when pumping. Of course, this practice resulted in spills and overall inconvenience, necessitating the need for a more accurate method. As a stop-gap measure until the new technology could be implemented, many stations passed out wooden "dipsticks" that allowed curious automobilists a more practical method of checking fuel level. Unfortunately, automotive tanks were not any sort of standard size, accounting for the often confusing set of scales found on these crude instruments. *White Eagle Antique Mall Collection*

The Teapot Dome Station Hut, Zilla, Washington
The "Teapot Dome" oil scandal of 1923 was a dark day for this nation's petroleum refiners as well as the administration of President Warren G. Harding. A Senate investigation uncovered that Secretary of the Interior Albert Fall had persuaded Secretary of the Navy Edwin Denby to transfer government oil reserves located at Teapot Dome, Wyoming, and Elk Hills, California, to the Department of the Interior. Mr. Fall then leased these reserves to private petroleum producers E.L. Doheny and Harry Sinclair. Absolutely no competitive bidding of any kind was involved, and the subsequent lease deals were illegally secured by the refiners with large amounts of money. As a tongue-in-cheek reminder of those infamous days, a quaint gasoline station shaped like a teapot takes care of motorists in Zilla, Washington. For the average motorist unschooled in the history of the American gas station, it's just another crazy roadside attraction vying for its share of the gasoline trade.

denly became an integral part of the service station marketing scheme.

To keep customers from patronizing other shops, stations also consolidated repair bays, lubritoriums, and tire services under one roof. Even gasoline pumps became part of the all-out merchandising effort. New fuel dispensers featured glass cabinets capable of housing motor oils, anti-freeze, head lamps, cables, and other automotive gadgetry.

Keeler's Korner, Lynnwood, Washington
Tall gasoline pumps with clear glass crucibles towered over Highway 99 when Keeler's Korner first opened in 1927. In those early days of the automobile, Carl Keeler pumped the gasoline himself and never once failed to check the oil level in the customer's crankcase. Back then, traveling over the highways and byways of rural America was still quite enjoyable. Enthusiastic automobilists (ain't we got fun) bent on experiencing all the joys of the motorcar delighted in taking even the smallest of journeys. Simple pleasures still prevailed. The journey itself was the focus of almost every trip, and the destination less important than the fun and adventure to be had along the way! To this day, a pair of slender red pump dispensers still draw the curious to old man Keeler's quaint green and white building in Lynnwood, Washington. Although gasoline is no longer sold here, the pleasant memories and rich recollections to be savored at Keeler's Korner are absolutely free.

As the end of the thirties approached, new station structures incorporated elements of Streamline Moderne. Decorative pylons, speed lines, curved corners, neon tubing, and portholes provided an illusion of speed. At long last, filling stations and

113

Tony's Tank Standard Station, circa 1930
During the 1930s, station attendants were always on alert for the motorist. This Standard Oil outlet featured a women's restroom, three Wayne 60 gasoline dispensers, Pyro Anti-Freeze, Mobiloil, Esso lubrication products, Kyso gasoline, and of course—ice-cold Coca-Cola in bottles. If only today's station attendant looked so alert! *Courtesy Caufield & Shook Collection, Photographic Archives, University of Louisville. Neg.# CS 155188*

roadways became mutually complimentary. For a brief period in the timeline of the American gas station, commercial refueling structures attained their purest form: not Grecian monuments, Chinese Pagodas, nor country cottages ... but highly specialized businesses geared to refilling automobiles with gasoline.

Commercial Pumper House, Fredonia, Kansas
Early gasoline refueling structures were simply glorified sheds and other makeshift structures. To remain competitive and attract motorists, petroleum companies learned that a more dignified image had to be portrayed. As a result, a number of refiners chose to fashion their station buildings in the familiar house format. Pure Oil and Phillips constructed many of these cottage gasoline outlets, practically bringing the safe and secure feeling of home to the American roadways. For the oil marketer, the quaint form held another attraction: Because the house fit in so well and in some cases was regarded as an "architectural asset," restrictive zoning ordinances and construction bans were often eased. Accepted as one of the most popular forms of architecture for gas sales, the English cottage was readily accepted for installation in most suburban communities during the twenties. With its newfound respect, the gasoline station could be constructed virtually anywhere a roadside lot was available—including residential areas.

Chevron Station With Attendants, circa 1940s
During the 1940s, the responsibility of filling an automobile gasoline tank with motor fuel, checking the engine oil level, and cleaning the windshield fell on one person: the service station attendant. Dressed in company uniform and almost always wearing an eight-point garage cap, the friendly neighborhood pump operator was widely respected as America's automotive sage. When it came to gasoline grades, he knew it all. If a tire was flat and needed repair, he patched it—right on the spot. Lubrication viscosity, mile-per-gallon, and tire rotation were all subjects he (and sometimes she) could offer advice about. Regardless of his technical prowess or mechanical ability, the service station attendant wasn't afraid of hard work, checking the oil, and wiping the windshield. *Photograph provided, and reprinted with permission, by Chevron Corporation and its subsidiary, Chevron U.S.A. Inc., Hand-tinting by Michael Karl Witzel.*

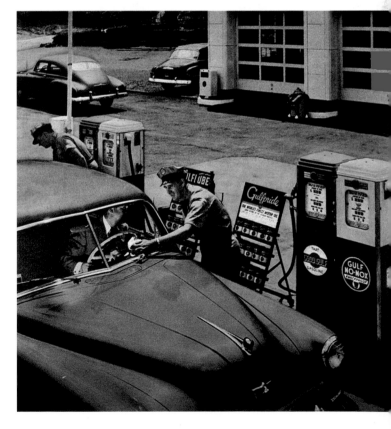

Neon Station Clock

During the heyday of the American gas station, the Electric Neon Clock Company of Cleveland, Ohio, produced a number of beautiful clocks for use in service stations and other commercial roadside structures. Long before digital electronics transformed timepieces into impersonal chronometers, colorful rings of bright neon outlining bold analog clock-dials ruled the roadsides. Restaurants used them as centerpieces above their Formica counters and gas station owners proudly mounted them above the office door. Along with the familiar red Coke machine and the mirror-front cigarette machine, these colorful clocks were an accepted part of the average gas station scene. But, like everything else familiar that is quickly taken for granted, the classic neon clock fell from popularity with nary a whimper. Today, only a scarce smattering of these precious survivors remains—awaiting their rediscovery—and eventual rebirth.

Opposite page, bottom
Standard Oil Service Station, 1949
Standard Oil of California operated a number of
eye-catching stations on the West Coast during the
late '40s. Station attendants dressed in pure white
conveyed a positive image to the motorist and helped
to diminish the "grease monkey" reputation some
auto service men inadvertently promoted. *Photograph
provided, and reprinted with permission, by Chevron
Corporation and its subsidiary, Chevron U.S.A. Inc.*

Phillips 66 Full Service, 1952
The true story of the Phillips company trademark
began when the first gallon of gas was offered to the
motoring public in Wichita, Kansas, on November 19,
1927. Phillips was venturing into the consumer market,
their goal being to offer a fuel superior to any currently
sold. In the frenzy to perfect their product, Phillips
delayed selecting the right imagery to represent the
new gas until the last minute. A special executive
committee session was organized for the sole purpose
of coming up with a new trademark. On the night of
the meeting, a Phillips company official was returning
to headquarters in Bartlesville in a company car being
used to test the new Phillips gasoline. "This car goes
like 60 on our new gas," the official exclaimed. "Sixty
nothing," answered the driver, glancing at the
speedometer, "we're doing 66!" The next day at the
conference the incident was reported. Somebody
asked where this actually occurred and the answer
came back: "Near Tulsa on Highway 66." That locked
it up! "Phillips 66" did sound pretty catchy. A vote was
put to the committee and the decision came back
unanimous. The new banner under which the Phillips
Petroleum Company would launch its line of gasolines
would be none other than "Phillips 66." The Phillips
66 trademark is viewed as one of the most widely
recognized corporate symbols representing automotive
fuels in America. Numerous amusing stories and
unbelievable explanations have sprung up over the
years attempting to explain the origin of this distinctive
logo. While some of these stories are based on facts,
others remain mired in myth. Still, many of these yarns
have found their way into the folklore of the American
service station and continue to be passed along by
the average motorist—unaware of the real facts and
circumstances. (Circa 1952). *Courtesy Corporate
Archives, Phillips Petroleum Company*

**Abandoned Roadside Station,
Mannford, Oklahoma**
These days, classic station scenes from our roadside
past are becoming more and more infrequent.
Vintage Pepsi-Cola and Dr. Pepper signs like these
are now treasured collectibles, along with the
particular visible register unit still intact within this
frame. Taken by photographer Harold Corsini in
1946 for Standard Oil of New Jersey, this Mannford,
Oklahoma, refueling stop has seen its share of use.
*Courtesy Standard Oil (New Jersey) Co. Collection,
Photographic Archives, University of Louisville.
Neg.# SONJ 34845*

Phillips 66, Anchorage, Alaska, 1967

One of the more bizarre stories perpetuated to explain the origin of the Phillips trademark is that a company official won the company's first Texas Panhandle refinery in a dice game! The previous owner rolled "double-sixes" in an unlucky toss and lost it all! Back over the border in Bartlesville, company directors liked those unlucky boxcars so much that they decided to name the refinery's gasoline product "Phillips 66." In reality, this story originates from the Texas refinery's infamous neighbor, (the 6666 Ranch) reportedly won in a poker game with a hand of four sixes. It's a tall Texas tale, as fanciful as those describing Jackalopes and giant armadillos. (Circa 1967). *Courtesy Corporate Archives, Phillips Petroleum Company*

Stone Station Man and Pumps, Seattle, Washington

Jack Collier fondly remembers the days when his father first opened his stone gasoline station. Back then, American cars like the Packard 120 and Ford Model "A" dominated Rainier Avenue. Tall visible register gas pumps were the current trend in dispensing equipment, indicative of the latest technology. Pumped by hand crank or electric motor, powerful motor fuel would slowly fill a glass cylinder, then drain by way of gravity into the automobile gas tank. Since pumping gas was a much slower process than present day, time was plentiful for simple services like checking the oil and pressure in the tires. When problems surfaced, station mechanics assisted with even the smallest of mechanical repairs—and why not? When hoods were pulled away, simple mechanisms offered little challenge for the experienced pump jockey handy with a wrench.

FOR EVERYTHING YOUR CAR NEEDS—

Chapter 2

ATTENDANTS

During the golden age of the American service station, attendants played a pivotal role. As highly visible employees, pump operators were an extension of the brand sold. To ensure return business, their appearance had to instill a sense of quality in the mind of the motorist. Along with gasoline, the motorist was buying an image.

As gas stations became more standardized across America, the grease-monkey became an embarrassment. Oil refiners wanted to cultivate a national image and eliminate the tumble-down gasoline shacks of the early 1900s. Station employees were required to don uniforms.

Like their well-dressed counterparts in the military, the pump jockeys had to look sharp at all times. Polished leather shoes and matching shin guards became part of the new look. Jodhpur trousers worn with a matching waist-jacket were now an important part of the basic uniform as was the crisp black bow-tie.

To pull together the unified station image, the petroleum company insignia was displayed on the breast pocket of the uniform. Fashioned in the form of a metal pin or fabric patch replicating the larger sign

Mobil Station Service Attendant
As a mythical figure of the great American roadside, the service station attendant towered above them all. As depicted in this Mobil advertisement, the attendant was indeed a larger than life figure in the mind of many an automobile owner. From coast to coast, in the big cities, small towns, and even on remote highways, he was someone to turn to in a time of need. For him, pumping gasoline, checking the oil level, and making sure that the windshields were clean was only a small part of the job. Relating to people on a one-to-one basis with friendliness and compassion was much more important. The physical embodiment of the American work ethic, pioneering spirit, and "can-do" attitude, the gasoline service station attendant was at one time an important element of the roadside tapestry. We look back to these gas pumping giants with fondness, hoping for their eventual return. *Courtesy Mobil Oil Corporation*

Rose Street Attendants, Seattle, Washington

Today, only miles from the historic Seattle site where John McLean erected one of America's first filling stations, Wally Hilde continues the full-service tradition. His eager-to-satisfy team of attendants jockey to refuel cars and skillfully repair the mechanical components that keep them moving. Service men Rodger, Juan, and Ramiro routinely infuse a healthy dose of customer service into their daily tasks—the same brand of friendliness once found at the gasoline businesses of days past. At Rose Street Auto, there are no self-service pump dispensers or faceless "attendants" cloistered behind plexiglass. Real personalities take care of customers. For all concerned, it makes the all-too-frequent routine of pulling off the fast-track to have one's gas-tank filled or oil checked a more pleasant experience. Hilde learned a long time ago that the type of relationship a business has with its patrons is what brings them back, regardless of the chemical properties of gasoline sold or the technology used to pump it from underground tanks. The most expensive facilities and equipment cannot, and never will, compensate for a basic lack of customer service.

FULL BODY

CLEAN·CLEAR·PURE

"*Still plenty of oil-and body O.K.!*"

That's the answer thousands of motorists receive who use Texaco Golden Motor Oil regularly. Even after a long, hard vacation trip this pure golden oil still clings to the "stick"—still retains that famous full body which assures many more miles of safe, care-free driving.

Texaco is specially refined from carefully selected crudes *only*, with a scientific precision that no known process can improve. It is as golden pure as it looks. It is free from gummy residual tars which cause faulty valve action and sticking piston rings — free from gritty-carbon-forming elements which cause an engine to over-heat, falter and lose power.

For maximum summer motoring satisfaction stop consistently under the Texaco Red Star with the Green T. This symbol can be seen at convenient intervals along all our great national highways. The Lincoln Highway, for instance, is a Texaco Trail with Service Stations never more than an hour apart. Texaco is the only gasoline and motor oil sold in every one of our 48 States.

THE TEXAS COMPANY, TEXACO PETROLEUM PRODUCTS

TEXACO
GOLDEN MOTOR OIL

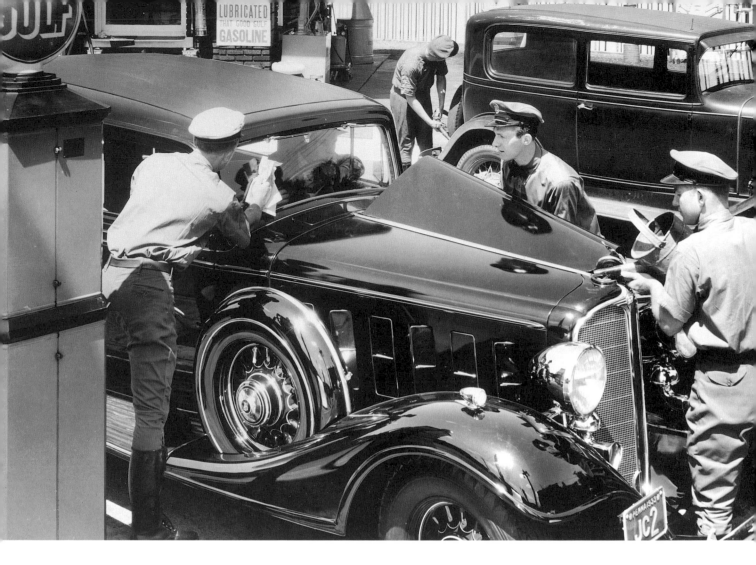

Previous page

Texaco Body Still O.K. Motor Oil

"Still plenty of oil—and body O.K.! That's the answer thousands of motorists receive who use Texaco Golden Motor Oil regularly. Even after a long, hard vacation trip this pure golden oil still clings to the stick—still retains that famous full body which assures many more miles of safe, care-free driving." In the innocent days of motoring, motor lubricants were comprised of relatively simple blends of refined petroleum. With the fields of oil production and chemical engineering still in their infancy, limited criteria were available to analyze refined products. Thermal breakdown and viscosity were terms for the future. Clean, clear, and pure dominated the printed page. *Courtesy Texaco Inc.*

Three Attendant Service Lives

Imagine pulling into a gasoline station and having your car serviced by three station attendants! For today's jaded motorist, it's the stuff dreams are made of. However, during the thirties it was no dream: Gulf stations like this example sold No-Nox Ethyl from clock-faced pumps for fourteen and a half cents per gallon. Wiping the windows, checking the oil, and topping off the fluid in the radiator was all part of the deal. (Circa 1933). *Photograph provided, and reprinted with permission, by Chevron Corporation and its subsidiary, Chevron U.S.A. Inc.*

Can I Fill Your Tank, Mister?

Lillian Larsen was one of Standard's most able station attendants during 1942. Serving the road as an important asset to the war effort, female pump operators like her became a familiar sight at the American service station. While husbands, brothers, fathers, and cousins were battling it out for our freedom (to drive when and where we wanted), wartime gasoline stations continued to operate with as much normalcy as they could. *Photograph provided, and reprinted with permission, by Chevron Corporation and its subsidiary, Chevron U.S.A. Inc.*

Selling Furniture Polish

A service station attendant points out a new furniture polish product to a female customer at a Phillips' service station during the early 1930s. To augment revenues in the days of economic downturn, petroleum refiners manufactured a number of products for sale at company stations. The American housewife was now quite adept at the controls behind the wheel and had quickly become a major economic force to be reckoned with. Furniture polish, glass cleaner, insect spray, and a number of other fluids were routinely marketed to the modern woman—right along with gasoline and oil. The station attendant often acted as an ad hoc salesman for many of these goods, giving friendly advice for their use. The time spent at the pumps provided the perfect opportunity to win over new customers. *Courtesy Corporate Archives, Phillips Petroleum Company*

Socony Attendant's Hat
Like the military man, firefighter, police officer, and postal worker, the service station attendant of the not too distant past always wore some type of head covering while pumping gas and performing related automotive tasks. Simple cloth caps were some of the first worn by station employees, followed by the black-brimmed variety much like those already adopted by numerous government service organizations. For the most part, these multi-pointed head-toppers were an image accessory—company trademarks and related brand insignias quickly attained prominence on the frontal region of the filling station chapeau. Colorful oil company logos were routinely mounted above center brim—tying together the "unified look" so intensely desired by most of the truly competitive oil concerns. The resulting look commanded attention, respect, and trust. It's no wonder that Texaco's famous slogan, "You can trust your car to the man who wears the star," was so effective in recruiting customers.
White Eagle Antique Mall Collection

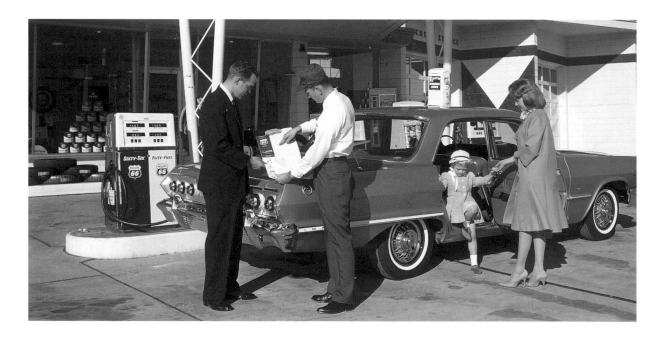

Phillips 66 Stations For Families, circa 1950s
A few scientifically oriented scenarios have been perpetuated to explain the origins of the Phillips 66 name, including the unfounded tale that Phillips gasoline was sixty-six octane and that its famous "controlled volatility" feature was perfected after sixty-six laboratory tests. Unfortunately, no one really knows for sure how many actual laboratory tests were conducted to perfect the controlled volatility of "Phillips 66" gasoline. Furthermore, the technical methods for determining gasoline octane rating wouldn't even be adopted until five years after the original Phillips trademark was selected! (Circa 1950s).
Courtesy Corporate Archives, Phillips Petroleum Company

Station Attendant's Patches

Since the first gallon of gas was sold at the American filling station, the pump attendant has acted as a highly visible product representative. When motoring was still young, excited vehicle owners cared little about how the pump or depot operator was dressed. Finding gasoline was the main concern. Yet, as gasoline locomotion became more refined, standard uniforms slowly replaced stained overalls—the attire of the average gas station employee slowly evolved into a highly refined costume. To identify the pump jockey and to differentiate the brand of gas sold, insignias were permanently affixed to hats, shirts, and jackets. While the attendant pumped gas, checked oil, or wiped the windshield, the customer would see a constant reminder of exactly what brand he was purchasing. Extremely colorful, eye-catching, and often humorous, the embroidered gasoline patch was the original predecessor of today's designer label.
Walter Webber Collection

Lil' Phil Attendant Doll
Well aware that gasoline station collectibles are now desired by a vast market interested in nostalgia, the Phillips Petroleum Company has recently licensed a toy manufacturer to issue number one in a series of station attendant dolls. Capturing all of the whimsy contained in the original version manufactured years ago, it comes complete—packaged with a light brown Phillips' signature attendant's uniform and black-brimmed cap. While the service station attendant many motoring Americans came to know and love during the golden age of the automobile may no longer be a reality, the magic of those former days may be recaptured with one of these commemorative dolls.

Phillips Attendant Award
As an incentive to sell gasoline, portray a positive public image, and perform quality maintenance work, many oil companies bestowed awards upon their best station attendants. Phillips Petroleum of Bartlesville, Oklahoma, utilized this commanding rendition of a service employee to honor many of their top gasoline station personnel during the 1960s. Embodying the bold styling of machine age imagery with its cubist design, this golden statuette was the equivalent of a Hollywood Oscar in the world of the service station worker. Highly prized by any station attendant worth his salt, company service awards were an important aspect of building employee character. By reinforcing the idea of customer satisfaction and adherence to quality with these awards, petroleum refiners succeeded in creating a valuable pool of automotive servers. *Red Horse Museum Collection*

near the roadway, it confirmed company identity for the motorist.

Influenced heavily by the style of military uniforms, a hat typical of any "serviceman" adorned the head. Decorated with the same company identification as the jacket, it strengthened brand recognition during face to face interactions with the public.

Eventually, oil companies relaxed styles at their stations and utilized the basic jumpsuit as uniform. Covering the legs, arms, and major portions of the body, it was the perfect shell for protection against grease and dirt. The bow-tie remained standard and soft caps made from matching fabric covered the head.

Still, a uniform mode of dress and pleasant appearance wasn't the last word in customer satisfaction. Personalities became an important issue, along with a willingness to do the job right the first time and please the customer during his or her brief visit. In the days of the Packard and Duesenberg, the customer was always right.

With a courteous smile and friendly demeanor, service station attendants were expected to carry out the basic rituals

Mobil Window Spray
One of the major attractions of full service gasoline stations used to be the simple procedure of having one's windshield cleaned. Long before the engineers in Detroit even thought of spraying cleaning fluid up through tubes mounted under the windshield, the task of wiping glass clean was the exclusive domain of America's service station attendants. The standard tools of the trade to accomplish this complimentary task included the hand-held spray bottle, rubber squeegee, and lint-free shop towel. As the gallons rang out from the pump, motorists relaxed in the front seat as every trace of bugs, mud, and road film was eradicated from the glass. Watching the process proved fascinating: there was a definite technique required to perform the task efficiently, mixed with individual flair and occasional braggadocio. For those who wanted to experiment with this "service" art and try their hand at cleaning their own wind screen, Mobil offered small bottles of glass cleaner to take home. *White Eagle Antique Mall Collection*

required to ensure motoring safety and pleasure. Checking the oil and tire pressure were a large part of the job, as was checking mechanical components under the hood for signs of impending failure. Making sure the windshield was free from dirt and insects were high on the list of station chores.

When an automobile first pulled up to the pumps, the station attendant was always there to greet it. Without hesitation, the eager-to-please attendant pleasantly inquired to the amount of gasoline desired and set about the task of operating the pump. While the fuel flowed into the tank, the pump man wasted no time daydreaming. Customers were enlightened to the different grades of motor oil, automotive questions were answered, free maps and prizes were handed out, and road directions clarified.

With flawless choreography, the skilled service station attendant could complete all of these tasks, debate the chance for rain, and make it back to the filler hose with time to spare. The tank would be full, all without spilling a drop of gasoline.

Phillips Attendant Filling, 1965

One of the most common stories explaining the use of the "66" designation is that company founder Frank Phillips was sixty-six years old when he formulated the Phillips Petroleum Company. This is far from the truth, as Mr. Phillips came into this world in the year 1873 and was only forty-four years old when the company first incorporated on June 13, 1917. "Phillips 44" would have made a rather uninteresting company trademark! Another mix-up with numbers takes the form of the first-day-of-sales story. In this version, the flagship Phillips station had sold exactly 6,600 gallons of gasoline by the end of the first day's business. Supposedly, the station operator turned to a company official (who just happened to be standing nearby) and exclaimed: "Boy, 66 is our lucky number!" This could be possible, if it weren't for the fact that Phillips' first Wichita gasoline station sold 12,000 gallons that historic day. Many patrons had free five-gallon coupons, too, further reducing the quantities actually paid for. (Circa 1965). *Courtesy Corporate Archives, Phillips Petroleum Company*

Wayne Pumps Measure Gas by the Penny's Worth

.... to Guarantee Full Value for Every Cent you Pay

IF YOU NEEDED gasoline, how many gallons could you order if you had just 80c to spend? No need to figure...just say *"80c worth, please"* and a modern Wayne Pump will fill your order to the last full penny's worth.

Modern Waynes, *the Watchdogs of your Gasoline Dollar*, measure gasoline by the penny's worth as well as the gallon ... eliminate price figuring, "eye measure" and other sources of error ... *guarantee* you Honest Measure ... and let you order by the gallon, tankful or dollar's worth, whichever you prefer.

Waynes can't make a mistake ... can't over-charge you. *With unfailing accuracy*, Wayne's patented precision meter tallies each fraction of a gallon *as it goes into your tank*. And automatically, with split-penny accuracy, Wayne's amazing mechanical brain totals the cost, cent by cent, before your eyes.

Wherever you see them, Wayne Pumps mark dealers who put your interest first. Waynes can't be started until the dials are set to zero. *They are accurate at full flow or a trickle.* They can fill your tank to the top without spilling a drop.

So look for the Wayne name and "Honest Measure" seal ... your guarantee of accuracy.

See YOUR Soldier!
Visit His Camp ... By Car

Wayne Pump
The Watchdog of your Gasoline Dollar

Your soldier boy will be mighty glad to see faces from home . . . and you'll be happy to see for yourself how well he's looking, too. So plan to go soon for at least a quick visit with him, and a look at the new defenses he's helping build for America. And make the trip by car!

All the way, you'll find modern service stations waiting like familiar friends to meet every motoring need . . . to provide efficient, speedy service, maps, road information, clean rest rooms . . . everything they can offer to make your journey easy and pleasant.

THE PUMP COMPANY...FORT WAYNE, INDIANA

World's Largest Manufacturer of Gasoline Pumps ... Est. 1891

Chapter 3

PUMPS

Sylvanus F. Bowser designed the first workable gasoline pump in 1885. Initially intended to pump coal oil, it was later modified to deliver gasoline. By 1905, it was housed within a wooden storage cabinet and dubbed a "filling station" by Bowser salesman Jake Gumpper. Easy to operate, this self-measuring storage pump marked a new age for commercial fuel dispensing.

As more effective methods replaced the depot methods of tin can, chamois, and funnel, radical pump refinements followed. By 1906, John J. Tokheim perfected a compact visible and cylinder-measuring pump featuring a water-separating glass dome. Six years later, Gilbert & Barker introduced the T-8 one-gallon hand pump. Technologically superior to previous models, it was capable of delivering fifteen gallons of fuel per minute. Still, disreputable operators could rig the dial indicator to produce false readings.

As a result, the public came to view these "blind" pumps with a suspicious eye. Unable to monitor what was really flowing through the filler hose, gasoline purchasers

Wayne Honest Measure Gas Pumps
With the introduction of the mechanical calculator pump in 1932, the Wayne Pump Company gained the confidence it needed to guarantee the customer full value for every cent they paid. The eye-measurement of the visible register pumps suddenly became outmoded, as did the large dial indicators of the clock-face pumps. Freed from the mental chore of having to figure out how many gallons could be purchased for a specific monetary amount, gasoline could be sold by increments as small as a penny! The days of purchasing motor fuel by the gallon were over and a new era of customer confidence ushered in. Unfortunately, the majority of pump companies tried to dismiss the new device as something they didn't really need. Still, as more and more stations tried the new units, their popularity spread. Soon, dealers across the country demanded the advanced pumps. A few pump manufacturers introduced their own calculators, but were soon taken to court by Wayne for patent infringement. When the dust finally settled, most manufacturers of gasoline dispensers signed licensing agreements with the Wayne Pump Company.
Courtesy Wayne Pump Company

MODEL 214

PORTABLE GASOLINE TANK

WITH
GALLON MEASURING PUMP

MODEL 214 Portable Unit is approved and labeled by The Underwriters' Laboratories, Inc., and is designed for safely and conveniently serving Gasoline in Garages, Service Stations, Automobile Storage or Sales Buildings, Factories and wherever stationary equipment is not advisable.

This method of handling gasoline has some advantages. When used indoors it facilitates the filling of cars without moving or shifting them, and it can be placed on the elevator and taken from floor to floor. When used at the curb it can readily be pushed indoors at night. It is sturdy and substantial and will stand severe service.

TOKHEIM OIL TANK AND PUMP COMPANY
FORT WAYNE, INDIANA, U. S. A.
Designers and Manufacturers of Complete Gasoline and Oil Dispensing Equipment

BULLETIN No. 159

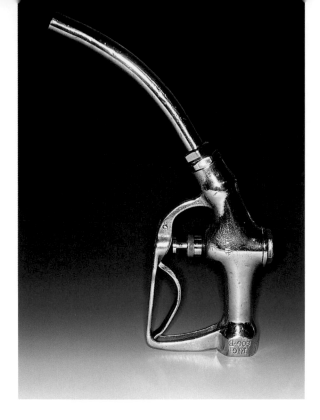

Brass Pump Handle

Gasoline pump nozzles like this brass Buckeye model were once beautiful works of utilitarian machinery. Before the advent of the information age, visual aesthetics still played an important role in the design of products, machinery, and household objects. Albeit many of these designs were considered modern for their time, they still contained that subtle hint of craftsmanship that makes an object more than the sum of its parts. Unlike today's smaller aluminum models (coated with plastic shrouds and various rubber accessories to trap vapors), these substantial valve spouts were an indispensable part of the helpful service station attendant's refueling arsenal. With pump nozzle in hand, standing at attention at the pump dressed in full-dress regalia, yesterday's gasoline station attendant was a roadside sight to behold.

Model 214 Portable Tank

The Tokheim Model 214 portable gasoline tank was a handy accessory for the early marketer of streetside gasoline. With a gallon measuring pump and internal fifty gallon storage tank, this unit could be moved easily (with its 30in wheels) to the curbside in order to service automobiles. With its use, general stores, drugstores, hardware establishments, repair facilities, and other business not normally geared to serving the motorcar with fuel could readily sell gasoline to its regular customers. One stroke of the plunger provided a full gallon, with selective stops provided for half-gallon, quart, and pint measure. A 10ft hose supplied with the unit allowed automobile gasoline tanks to be filled directly. *Courtesy Tokheim Corporation*

were highly dubious of accurate measurement and purity.

To placate beleaguered petroleum refiners and to discourage cheating, manufacturers soon introduced improved pump models. Securely mounted on top of a tall support made from heavy iron, a round glass cylinder now held gasoline in plain sight. Within the transparent crucible, graduated markers measured gas volume–plainly "registering" the amount readied for sale.

Unfortunately, the possibilities for dishonesty were not eliminated by the visible register design. A strategically placed brick could falsely inflate the measurement inside the glass cylinder. Gallon markers could easily be misaligned. Accurate readings were difficult from close angles, often rendering the motorist's view through the windshield a disadvantage.

By the close of the twenties, electric meter pumps joined the visibles on the roadside. Oversized "clock face" indicators displayed the quantity delivered on these new arrivals as a bell signaled the delivery of every gallon.

The Wayne Pump Company introduced the first calculator pumps in 1932, permanently altering the way Americans purchased gasoline. With a "Head for Figures,"

Cut 650
Manually Operated Five-Gallon Capacity Continuous Recording Pump
Equipped with Combination Hose Air Release Valve and Tele-Gauge
Speedy—Compact—Simple—Accurate—Symmetrical

Compact and symmetrical in design, this new Tokheim Five-Gallon Capacity Pump effectively fulfills every requirement for the speedy, accurate dispensing of gasoline either at the Curb or in Filling Stations.

The operation of Cut 650 requires no back-cranking, simply a continuous forward motion of the crank, which reverses the plunger at any point desired and returns it to the bottom of the stroke at a greatly increased speed. Selective quantity stops are provided for one, two, three, four and five gallons. Combination hose air release valve and tele-gauge visibly indicates whether or not the pump is in prime and insures a smooth, rapid flow of gasoline to the fuel tank of the car. The continuous recording meter—to 1,000,000 gallons and repeating—enables an accurate check to be kept on all sales. Two large continuous recording dials—located on opposite sides of the pump—afford double protection to both the customer and operator. A positive bell ringing attachment audibly indicates the delivery of each completed gallon.

This pump is approved by the Underwriters' Laboratories, Inc., and bears their label.

Tokheim Oil Tank and Pump Company
FORT WAYNE, INDIANA, U. S. A.
Offices in Principal Cities

Third Ed. 2M—1-29.

Bennett 373-B With Clock Face
By the late '20s, electric meter pumps replaced the visible units at many gasoline stations. Aptly dubbed "clock-face" dispensers, these dial units were first developed by L.O. and N.A. Carlson of Erie Meter Systems and replaced the fragile glass tank of the visible register pump for gasoline measurement. Whether flowing at fifteen gallons per minute or just one drop at a time, the new pumps boasted increased accuracy. Advanced units such as the Bennett 373-B were simpler to operate and safer than the hand-operated visible pumps. Unfortunately, these attractive "timepieces" were eventually replaced by even more practical calculator dispensers. *Courtesy Bennett Pump Company*

Cut 650 Gasoline Pumps
The Cut 650 was 1927's answer to the gasoline pump. A manually operated unit, it pumped gasoline with the continuous forward movement of a single hand crank. On each side of its symmetrical body, two large recording dials provided the means for customer and station operator to see how much gasoline was pumped, with a side-mounted "tele-gauge" provided for visual inspection of gasoline and prime condition. A long flexible filler hose, still lacking any sort of nozzle valve, provided the conduit for easy tank filling. As each gallon was cranked and delivered, an internal bell-ringing attachment provided the auditory signal. Tokheim supplied generic, round "Gasoline" globes to their 650 customers, and finished the standard model in a bright red enamel. *Courtesy Tokheim Corporation*

their mechanical computers radically transformed the entire pump industry. Eventually, competing pump manufacturers were forced to license the patented technology for their own pumps. Existing units were rendered obsolete—overnight.

Now, instead of reading a dial indicator for the total gallons and consulting a corresponding price chart, the operator simply glanced at the calculated price. For the first time in the history of the American service

Six Assorted Gasoline Pumps

For the last fifty years, the gasoline dispenser has been largely ignored. When Model Ts rattled up and down Main Street, visible register pump units with glass crucibles and ornate metalwork captured the public's imagination. With the introduction of graceful gas pumps, the practice of filling the family car with fuel attained a marked measure of romance and new level of style. At the Don Garlits Museum of Drag Racing in Ocala, Florida, a number of these eye-catching pumps are currently on display. Gasoline pumps, identified from left to right: Fry Ten-Gallon Model 117 visible register (circa 1916–1923) with Mobilgas Special globe, Tokheim calculator pump (circa 1950s) with Blue Sunoco Capcolite globe, Erie clock face pump with Kendall one-piece globe, Gilbarco Calco-Meter Model 906-16G with Shell one-piece cast globe, National Model A-38 (circa 1945) with Dino Capcolite globe, Fry Ten-Gallon Model 117 visible register with Shell one-piece cast globe. *Marty Lineen, Jr. © 1993, Courtesy Don Garlits Museum*

Buy From a Fry
There's One Close By!

Gasoline sellers know the famous Fry Visible Pump develops confidence and attracts business because of its dependability.

That's the reason thousands of new Frys go into use every month.

You will find it both a pleasure and a satisfaction to buy your gasoline from a service station equipped with the Fry-Visible Pump.

The men in charge are dependable—so is their equipment.

Buy from a Fry—Millions do!

Guarantee Liquid Measure Co.
Rochester, Pennsylvania

PHILIP GIES PUMP COMPANY, Limited
Canadian Manufacturers and Distributors
KITCHENER, ONTARIO

Made in five and ten gallon capacities—both labeled by the Underwriters' Laboratories.

Always Accurate Fry Visible

With visible register pumps such as the Fry Model 117, gasoline was pumped from an underground tank by hand lever to fill a clear glass crucible. The round glass that gave the pumping device its name was securely mounted high atop a cylindrical support base made of heavy cast iron. Alongside the cylinder wall, graduated markers descending in numerical order from top to bottom gave indication of total volume. These gallon markers read out, or "registered" the amount of gasoline pumped from the ground and stored in the glass receptacle before sale. Unfortunately, the visible-register pumps were vulnerable to cheating, since markers could easily be misaligned. The contents of the crucible often expanded when the sun heated the glass, too—causing fuel to push through an overflow valve and back into the underground tank. During the summer, purchases had to be planned for the evening or other cool periods of the day in order to obtain the most gasoline for one's money.

station, the station attendant could confidently inquire: "Shall I fill 'er-up?"

As the silhouette of the American city changed, so did the appearance of the fuel dispenser. Pumps soon mirrored architectural forms in miniature, including the key structural components indicative of modern skyscrapers.

By the close of the thirties, the characteristics of streamlining began to soften the angularity of the fuel dispenser. Industrial designers influenced by the tapered bodies of aircraft integrated the look into new products. From cars to vacuums, contoured cowling soon enveloped the mechanism of almost every machine.

Finally, gasoline pumps portrayed the illusion of speed and efficiency. They were well on their way to the future—the digital brain and remote control just around the bend.

Bennett Red 646B Pump With Spinner
The smoothing characteristics of Streamlining began to hone away the sharp edges of the American gas pump by 1939 as many industrial designers were influenced by the parabolic tails and contoured bodies of aircraft. As the hard lines of the setback idiom began to soften, a more purified style of machine aesthetic was coming into vogue. Manufacturers redesigned everything from implements to appliances, improving functionality while incorporating modern styling. Electric refrigerators became aerodynamic, vacuum cleaners more swift, and gas pumps streamlined. Contoured cowlings covering mechanical components, transforming the fuel dispenser into a minimalist box—one that conveyed the static illusion of efficiency and speed to the passing motorist.
Courtesy Bennett Pump Company

THE *Bennett* 646 B

Chapter 4

GLOBES

The practice of mounting spherical shaped billboards on top of gas pumps began shortly after the first practical fuel dispensers were perfected. Pump manufacturers inaugurated the tradition by crowning some of their early blind units with attention-getting balls.

Wayne initially proffered a simple one-piece globe in 1912 to accompany their Cut 276 gasoline pump. Crafted from molded milk-glass, its primary function was to provide a distinctly decorative look. Perched high atop a tapered post, it lent an aura of respectability to what otherwise would have been a rather unattractive machine.

At that time, the majority of representations made by these unpretentious orbs were accomplished with simple generalities. "Filtered Gasolene" became the standard inscription—first painted, then etched into heavy globe glass. Other pump makers packaged similar globes with their new fuel dispensers, constraining the details of product dispensed within the boundaries of these universal descriptions.

While the horseless carriage was still a relatively new phenomenon, employing a generic designation to market motor fuel was still an acceptable practice. When an empty gasoline tank stranded the trailblaz-

Road Runner Racer
During the 1930s, a small independent Tulsa refiner began marketing gasoline under the Road Runner brand name. On glass globes produced for Dancinger between the 1930s and '40s, the large, elongated bird is displayed in rich detail—from its oversized bill to its long graduated tail. Suspended in mid-run, the reticent roadrunner aptly conveys the idea of swiftness. Four distinct gas pump globes were manufactured during this era, including Road Runner Regular, Road Runner Anti-Knock, Road Runner 400, and Road Runner Racer. The first three designs featured a detailed black and white roadrunner across the center of the globe face. The Road Runner Racer version displays the energetic bird on the lower portion of the globe. (Road Runner, 13.5in glass, repro inserts, plastic repro body). *Red Horse Museum Collection*

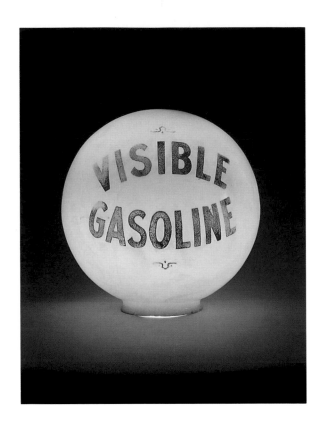

ing motorist along the skirt of the roadway, obtaining combustible fluid was all that mattered–regardless of who drilled, refined, and distributed it.

As the unprecedented proliferation of the motorcar boosted the demand for fuel, the gasoline industry maneuvered into the realm of big business. To secure their share of the lucrative market, competing refiners decided to make their distillations unique. Both major and minor oil concerns soon introduced customized globes depicting individual brands of gasoline.

With the inception of colorful graphics, stylized typography, and corporate insignias, once unbranded "gasoline" transcended from a generic commodity into a highly personalized liquid. Now readily associated with the visual symbols of purity, speed, superiority, and power–it quickly assumed a myriad of new identities within the competitive realm of the roadside.

The White Eagle division of Socony-Vacuum Oil capitalized on patriotic connections deeply rooted in national pride. By using a noble bird of prey for their fuel pump globe, they instantly conjured up feelings of patriotism and strength. At gasoline stations throughout Kansas and the Midwest, proud white birds kept a watchful eye

White Eagle Globe Blunt Nosed

The symbol of the white eagle—poised in noble assertion, and chosen for its representation as an oil company name, was first produced as a gas pump globe in 1924. This one-piece Eagle cast globe captured the vision of the stately raptor while providing the Kansas refiner with a powerful symbol, easily recognizable. The commanding atmosphere attained by a group of slender pumps topped with white eagles created a robust image for the White Eagle Oil and Refining Company—a look that set the company apart from its competitors. Regarded by many as the perfect corporate symbol, the majestic eagle received several embellishments between 1924 and 1932, producing four distinct globes: the blunt-nose, the slit-throat, and two versions of the pointed-nose. Despite their subtle differences, all contributed to the effect of stately dignity at company stations throughout the Midwest. White Eagle globes are largely distinguished by the variations in bill formation and feather details. With sparse body detail, the "blunt-nose" features a rounded bill, while the "pointed-nose" versions exhibit sharply curved bills. Feathers on the molded body are far more intricate than those on the blunt nose. A later model produced in 1932 boasts remarkable body detail, setting it apart from its other pointed-nose counterparts. In regards to body and style, the slit throat could be the twin of the blunt-nose, except for the casting line around the throat. (White Eagle Oil and Refining Company, cast one-piece glass, circa 1924–1932). *White Eagle Antique Mall Collection*

on the business of refueling.

Standard Oil of Indiana introduced three-dimensional versions of a majestic crown for their pumps. When seen from the roadway by motorists, these imperial markers transmitted positive messages of aristocracy and opulence. At twenty cents a gallon, customers pumping Stanolind's IsoVis gas knew they were getting a quality fuel!

145

Kanotex Bondified
Inspired by the "Sunflower State" nickname, Kanotex employed the seed-rich flower of Kansas on its globes long before it was adopted as part of the Kansas state flag in 1927. Originally Superior Refining, the Midwest oil enterprise trademarked its Kanotex name in 1909. A few years later, it began availing itself of one-piece etched globes to promote product. Although a few variations developed, these early globes featured a white star placed in front of a yellow sunflower, with oversized Kanotex "O." During the '30s, the company began using globes manufactured by the Gill Glass Company of Pennsylvania. Consisting of a hollow glass body with base, the Gill featured a narrow metal band on each side used to attach glass ad panels. These inserts were secured within the metal bands with the aid of an adjustable screw. Broken panels could now be easily replaced, enabling stations to maintain their globes without the added expense of total replacement. To further enhance the beauty of their globes, Gill later added a rippled texture to the glass body. Combined with baked-on paint inside, the Gill ripple globe gave off a most pleasing glow when internally illuminated. (Total Petroleum, Kanotex, Gill/rippled glass, circa 1930–1952). *Red Horse Museum Collection*

Unfortunately, the once ubiquitous gasoline pump globe has virtually disappeared from the American scene. Modern dispenser designs have rendered pump-top advertisements obsolete and impractical. On those rare pumps that have survived the change, the specter of vandalism and theft precludes any thought of their use.

All across the endless backroads of America—along small-town main streets, little known country roads, and two-lane highways—the friendly gasoline pump globes that once glowed brightly have dimmed. The tireless beacons consigned the duty of guiding motorists to safe harbor and favorite gasoline brands ... are just a memory.

Red Crown Chimney Cap

The practical refinement of the working light bulb was fraught with pitfalls. First, there was the problem of the fragile filament. Even after an osmium version was introduced in 1902, there was a problem with longevity (they burned out after fourty hours). As a result, early electric lamps were not very reliable until after the tungsten filament was introduced in 1906. However, the bulb still became extremely hot and had a penchant to explode when overheated. To accommodate these early difficulties, globe companies manufactured a one-piece glass globe that featured a 4in opening at its top. The collar of this hole was fitted with a small metal cap, acting as both vent and removable lid. Now, built-up heat could escape easily—while protecting the bulb from the rain. As lamps continued their all-too-rapid burn out, blackened bulbs could be easily replaced by station operators—without having to remove the entire globe from the pump. During the '20s, improvements in filament coils and the use of inert gases finally created longer lasting and safer bulbs. As a result, the chimney cap globe became obsolete. (Standard Oil Company of Indiana, Red Crown, used as light/dealer promotional piece, circa 1950s). *Red Horse Museum Collection*

Opposite page, bottom
Skelly and Stars

In 1919, William Skelly pooled his vast oil holdings and founded his own personal petroleum company—promptly naming the enterprise after himself. Perceiving a climate favorable to opportunity and growth, the flamboyant Oklahoma oil man eagerly purchased numerous service stations throughout the mid-continent states. If his gamble paid off, the financial rewards would be enormous. Unfortunately, Skelly's financial demise came swiftly on the heels of the great depression. Deeply in debt, he had no choice but to relinquish control of his brainchild to Standard Oil of New Jersey. At this point, Standard found itself in control of two separate oil entities, Skelly and Tidewater. To maintain its interests and to avoid a complete merger, it formed the Mission Corporation to oversee the pair. When the powerful J. Paul Getty later gained control of Tidewater, he received both oil concerns in the deal and by the 1960s, both companies officially merged with Getty. However, Skelly still held tenaciously onto its identity, stalling complete changeover to the Getty name until well into 1983. By this time, Texaco stepped in and purchased Getty—halting the process completely. Ironically, Skelly succumbed to rebranding in 1985—under the name of yet another owner: Texaco. So it goes in the soap opera of American Gas! (Skelly Oil Company, Skelly Gasoline, 13.5in glass, circa 1950–1956). *Red Horse Museum Collection*

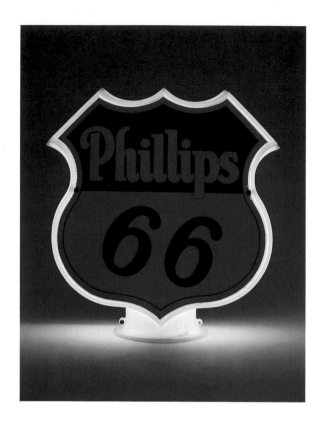

Phillips 66 Shield

When Adolph Spittler accidentally discovered casein plastics in 1897, the world was changed forever. Manufacturers, no longer limited to metal and glass, could now have durability, flexibility, and moldability—all in one product! Because this new plastic material could be dyed to any color during the manufacturing process, objects impervious to peeling or flaking could be readily created. As advancements were made, high heat and impact resistant acrylics, cellulose acetates, and polystyrenes went into full production by the 1930s—as did the globe manufacturers. In the forefront was the Cincinnati Advertising Products Company, of Cincinnati, Ohio. To hold glass inserts, their new plastic bodies came equipped with one screw topside and two near the base. Dubbed the "Capco," these lightweight globes were patented around 1932 and became exceedingly popular due to their durability. As the use of plastics flourished during the '50s, several manufacturers began creating unusually shaped three-piece globes. The Phillips 66 shield lent itself perfectly to this three-dimensional concept, resulting in the manufacture of two distinct models: Phillips 66 and the Phillips 66 Flite Fuel. (Phillips Petroleum Company, Phillips 66, all plastic shield, circa 1953–1959). *Dalton Patterson Collection*

Mobil Red Pump With Globe

In order to portray a more uniform brand name throughout its affiliate outlets, Socony and Vacuum (which merged in 1931) were determined to combine the Socony shield and Flying Red Horse with Vacuum's familiar "Mobilgas" brand. This conversion took many forms and was not accomplished completely until after WW II. The Magnolia and White Eagle divisions were among the first to adopt the new Mobilgas name, while others preferred to combine the Mobilgas brand designation with their own product names. As a result, globes depicting various brand names and logos—shown in concert with the Mobilgas name—proliferated. Since numerous manufacturers were involved with their design, a wide range of letter colors and type styles were seen at Socony-Vacuum affiliates, once they converted to Mobilgas. Interestingly enough, it was time for yet another rebranding in 1962 when the Mobilgas trademark was phased out.

The singular word "Mobil" replaced the old trademark, calling for replacement of gasoline pump globes one more time. Augusta, Kansas's Billie Butler has amassed quite an impressive collection of Socony collectibles. Her entire backyard is filled with Flying Red Horse signs and other Mobil memorabilia. A bright red restored Tokheim featuring a Mobilgas globe is one of her favorite pieces, occupying a position of prominence only a few feet from the edge of her backyard patio. While other neighbors play badminton and push lawnmowers through ankle high grass, Butler just sits back—takes a sip of iced tea, and admires all the colorful mementos she has acquired throughout the years. Not to be left out, husband Bob is a fan of the Flying Red Steed, too. He worked at the now defunct Mobil refinery for years and has acquired his own affection for anything and everything involved with the history of the company. *Billie Butler Collection*

Phillips
66
MOTOR OIL
PHILLIPS PETROLEUM COMPANY

ARCHER
LUBRICANTS
ONE U.S. QUART

Phillips
66
UNIQUE
MOTOR OIL

ONE U.S. QUART

EARLE
TROLEUM CO.
BRICANTS
Since 1889
TAIN MOTOR OIL
OMAHA
NEBR.

PHILLIPS
66
MM
MOTOR OIL

SKELLY
MOTOR
OIL
SKELLY OIL COMPANY

HEAVY
PRE
MOTO
PHILLIPS PET

custom-tailored
EXTRA HEAVY DUTY
RMAFILM
FOR A.P.I. SERVICE MS, DM
MOTOR OIL

TRADE MARKS REG. U.S. PAT. OFF. BY
OCONY MOBIL OIL COMPANY, INC.
LUBRITE
MOT

SKELLY
Skelly
Supreme
LOW CONSUMPTION
MOTOR OIL
HIGH V.I.-HEAVY DUTY

Chapter 5

CONTAINERS

When Colonel Drake first punched into a reservoir of Pennsylvania crude in 1859, the storage of raw oil posed a considerable dilemma. Since exploration took up considerable time and finances, transport and packaging logistics were often left for procrastination.

Luckily, the Titusville area played host to a number of breweries. Because most of them stocked an ample supply of wooden casks to store their spirits, brew masters soon found themselves inundated by frantic oil men searching for practical receptacles. With new oil reserves discovered daily, storage barrel construction soon proved more lucrative than drilling for rock oil.

While the wooden barrel provided the first link in the chain of bringing petroleum products to market, it was far from the final solution. To accommodate the filling stations that would flourish along the nation's roadways, improved packaging methods

would have to be developed.

Consequently, a variety of metal can motifs soon became standard for packaging retail auto-lubricants. Many of these oil vessels offered the convenience of a built-in pouring spout, while other designs provided

Oil Can Wall Frontal View
About twenty years ago, oil cans were generally regarded as throw-away items and were usually tossed in the trash. Those that did survive the final cut either ended up on the workbench holding screws or as a handy canister to clean dirty paint-brushes. As time progressed, a few forward thinking individuals realized that many of these tin containers featured pleasing graphics and corporate designs. Ever so slowly, a few eccentrics saved all the cans they could get their hands on and were soon scouring garbage dumps and other locations for new ones. As they worked on their new "hobby" in secret, the interest in nostalgia and filling stations increased. Suddenly, collecting oil cans was no longer a fringe activity! By the end of the eighties, desirability grew as values increased. For anyone interested in American road culture, the collecting of oil containers became serious business.
Red Horse Museum Collection

Mobiloil "A" Bottle Rack and Ford
When this 1937 Ford Tank Truck was hauling gasoline regularly, oil was often sold from clear glass decanters. A colorful rack often emblazoned with the brand name usually held eight of these bottles near a spot at the service island. The ever-ready station attendant would refill the clear one-quart containers with oil, hand-pumped from a bulk lubester capable of holding large quantities. To ensure that the customer was actually getting the quality they paid for, Mobil introduced their "Filpruf" containers. Featuring a patented spout requiring the use of a special gadget to remove it, they were filled with Mobiloil "A" at the local company bulk plant and delivered to stations for sale. (Before SAE numbers were used, different grades of oil were designated by petroleum refiners with letters. Mobil's "Guide to Lubrication" was one of the publications that outlined various grades, listing a number of formulas and their compatible make of automobile).
White Eagle Antique Mall Collection

Next page
Check the Oil Service
During the fifties, attendants at Phillips Petroleum stations made the simple procedure of "checking the oil" an integral part of the motorist's drive-in refueling ritual. Unlike the early days of the "filling station" when motor coach operators were basically on their own, vehicle owners themselves were encouraged to become part of the maintenance process. Crankcase dipsticks were readily shown to post-war customers as they were encouraged to learn all they could about their vehicle's upkeep. If the motorist himself could gain the confidence to identify oil that was breaking down, he would eventually return for an oil change and possibly the company's complete "Philcheck Service." Costly repairs would be avoided, Trop-Artic oil would be sold, and plenty of good will generated.
Courtesy Corporate Archives, Phillips Petroleum Company

a shaped metal flange to guide fluid. With the exception of cans introduced by Marathon in the shape of an oil derrick, screw-cap openings were almost universally positioned near the container's edge.

Later, a bent metal strap or heavy wire was attached to the top of these hand-soldered canisters to enable easy lifting. Rectangular full or half-gallon containers could readily be carried to a waiting motorcar by most customers.

At the same time, many gas stations sold oil from sixty-gallon bulk-dispensers positioned near the pump island. Glass bottles, usually stored in an eight container rack, were filled using the unit's small hand pump. "Fill-lines" molded into the clear bottlenecks provided the station attendant visual reference for exact quart measure.

Much to the chagrin of the public, the glass decanting method possessed gross inadequacies. Prior to the motorist's arrival, bottles could easily be filled with inferior oil, then represented as premium grade to the unsuspecting customer. As was the case with the visible register gas pumps, any visual reassurance obtained by the motorist provided a false security. Actually receiving honest measure—much less quality motor oil, wasn't always reality.

The same quandary applied to tin containers: because cans did not employ any sort of sealing device to indicate their prior opening, any disreputable seller could replenish empties with inexpensive product. Short of opening the containers upon delivery to check them, no method existed to confirm that oil purchased was actually the type and grade represented by the can label.

Eventually, a wave of allegations surfaced from a number of disgruntled sources.

Good Gulf Gasoline Pump Display
This Pittsburgh Gulf station relied heavily on Wayne display case pump dispensers during the year 1933. Although extremely fragile when it came to automobiles accidentally driving into them, these glass-cased units were the perfect salesman for every manner of car accessory. *Photograph provided, and reprinted with permission, by Chevron Corporation and its subsidiary, Chevron U.S.A. Inc.*

Retailers suspected of dishonesty reportedly were not selling trusted brands as advertised. Even the popular cartoon strip "Gasoline Alley" poked fun at the problem during the 1920s.

Well aware of the effect this kind of damaging press could have on business, petroleum refiners took serious notice.

Yellow Eight Car Can
The one-gallon rectangular can design was one of the earliest commercial oil vessels employed to market motor oil. Usually made of solid tin hand-soldered at the seams, these early canisters were often compact works of art. Taken for granted during their heyday as merely another form of commercial packaging, these square containers were often adorned with intricate designs. Free to embellish the metallic canvas of the oil can with engaging pictures, yesterday's unknown artists have left behind a pictorial history of packaging. During the height of their development, speedy racing cars, animals, and family sedans were the most frequent motifs employed. This one-gallon Eight Motor Oil (circa 1918) was a generic can sold to dealers and single stations empty. An operator could purchase one dozen at a time, fill them with oil, and pad stamp them to signify heavy, medium, or light grade. To unify the look of related products, identical cans were available in the one-gallon size, as well as grease containers holding one, five, and twenty-five pounds. *White Eagle Antique Mall Collection*

Expending considerable expense and effort, they continued to develop tamperproof packaging for motor oil. By the 1930s, most serious refiners switched to oil cans sealed at the source.

Soon, cylindrical metal tumblers filled with motor oil were sold at gas stations all across America. At long last, motorists could drive in, have the oil checked ... and be certain that the lubricants poured into their crankcases were "guaranteed to be refinery sealed!"

Oilzum Man Orange Can

The Oilzum man was an engaging trademark originated by the White & Bagley Company of Worcester, Massachusetts. Oilzum motor oils and lubrication products were quite popular during the '40s, touted on canisters as "America's Finest Motor Oils." Registered in the early 1900s as a protected product symbol, the Oilzum Man was one of America's first lubrication trademarks to become legally registered. Although quite appealing, the smirking visage was predestined for extinction from the first day it appeared on an oil can. Donning the protective headgear indicative of America's early motoring aficionados, Mr. Oilzum never failed to remind motorists of those early years. As Detroit's auto manufacturers produced more advanced machines for the post-war market, the American motorist looked increasingly towards the future—embracing the heavy chrome, streamlined fins, and modernity of the designs. Trademarks that glorified an age of antiquity quickly fell out of favor—rendered commercially impotent. In the gallery of the American marketplace, familiar characters like the Oilzum "dude" faded from prominence. Postscript: Oilzum was recently bought out by the Dryden Company of Baltimore, Maryland, and the White & Bagley headquarters in Massachusetts demolished. Believe it or not, Oilzum can still be bought in plastic bottles. *Tom Allen Collection*

Bow-tie Phillips Attendant Sells Oil

Another fanciful fable that hopes to explain the origin of the Phillips trademark is that Frank and L.E. Phillips, prior to founding the company, had only sixty-six dollars left when they struck their first successful well. Because of the timing, they decided that if they ever got to the point where they marketed gasoline it would be called "Phillips 66." This sounds believable, since the Phillips brothers were stretching their finances to the limit with their first oil explorations. After all, a fair number of dry holes were drilled by the pair prior to their first real gusher. But, whether or not they had a total of sixty-six dollars left between them when the well named Anna Anderson spouted black gold high into the Oklahoma night on September 6, 1905, cannot be confirmed by Phillips, or any other reliable historian. (Circa 1972). *Courtesy Corporate Archives, Phillips Petroleum Company*

NOW AT YOUR GULF DEALER'S _THE FINEST GULFPRIDE EVER!

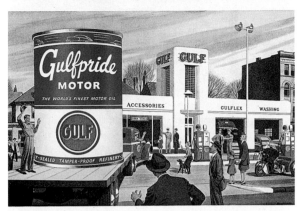

The new Gulfpride keeps your engine **running better** [Gulf scientists have found new ways to cut down oxidation, carbon, varnish, and to prevent foaming.] Gulfpride is the only motor oil that's Alchlor-processed [This is an extra refining step. It makes Gulfpride extra pure, extra free from sludge formation.] Get the new Gulfpride, the world's finest motor oil!

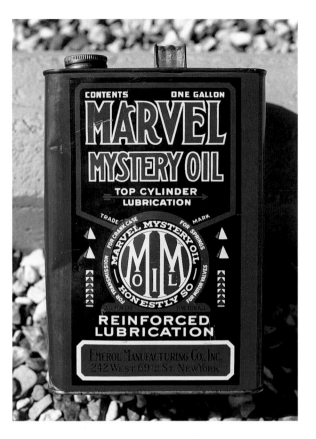

Gulfpride Motor Oil and Station

As increased competition and a depressed economy altered the carefree climate of gas and oil marketing during the early thirties (by 1933 there were over 170,000 gasoline stations doing business in the United States), automotive lubrication services and simple mechanical repairs were looked at from a fresh perspective. Soon, "lubritoriums" were built to satisfy the demand, with many existing stations adding on hydraulic lifts or grease pits. Eventually, Gulf Oil erected magnificent Streamline Moderne structures to market their "Gulflex" lubrication services, accessories, and exterior washing-all under one roof. The undignified filling station was growing up; the complete service station design becoming its welcome replacement. Refiners were proud of their new image and weren't afraid to show it—naming improved products such as motor oil accordingly. *Photograph provided, and reprinted with permission, by Chevron Corporation and its subsidiary, Chevron U.S.A. Inc.*

Marvel Mystery Oil

The Emerol Manufacturing Company of New York captured all of the ambiance of early "snake oil" salesmen with their unique oil can packaging. For the layman, assimilating many of the fantastic claims imprinted on the can had to be done with a grain of salt (maybe even a few dozen grains). Small pyramids, cryptic slogans, and a rather intriguing circular logo all lent an aura of the unknown to this unusual contender in the arena of multi-purpose lubricants. Supposedly, no one could really account for why this lubricant was "Slicker" than others (a secret additive?) and what unique process the company employed to manufacture it. Decades before the days of synthetic oil additives and other slippery chemicals were created in a laboratory test tube, this "mysterious" substance aided tremendously in Marvel's appeal. Yet even more amazing: Marvelous Mystery Oil is still sold in auto supply stores to this day! A willful survivor from the mid-teens, it's still packaged with the same eye-catching graphics and imagery as used on the earlier containers. *White Eagle Antique Mall Collection*

157

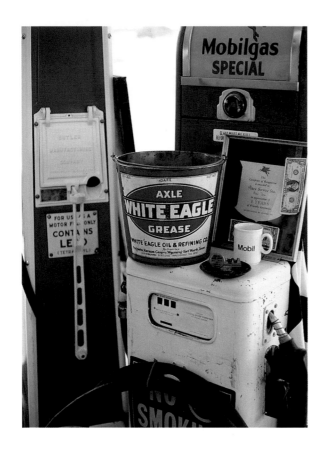

White Eagle Montage

In the year 1931, a basic grease job cost only fifty cents at a Standard Oil service station. If gear lubricant was needed in the transmission or differential, it cost fifteen cents per pound. When the warmer months of the year came around, both the transmission and differential would be drained of the 90 weight gear lube and replaced by 140 weight. For the station dealers it was a profitable ritual. Like the typical oil change, the profit margins were high. At the White Eagle Antique Mall in Augusta, Kansas, owner Bob McCalla displays many typical examples of the types of containers used to store these lubricants. When the motorcar was still young, grease buckets, such as this White Eagle "Dark" Axle Grease, were a common item stocked at the filling station. *White Eagle Antique Mall Collection*

Opposite
Texaco Sky Chief Gasoline

By the 1960s, petroleum companies developed new gasolines on a continual basis, many touting secret chemical additives or revolutionary refining processes. All claimed superior performance and quality, sometimes making it difficult for the motorist unschooled in the science of chemistry to discern exactly what was flowing into their automobile's tank. Texaco introduced their Sky-Chief brand and reinforced its climate-controlled qualities with a series of prints advertising in national publications. Specially blended to deliver top performance in each of the twenty-five weather areas in the United States, this "Volatane Control" motor fuel was just the ticket " for quick starts, fast warm-ups, smooth getaways, and power-a-plenty on the highways and up the hills." *Courtesy Texaco Inc.*

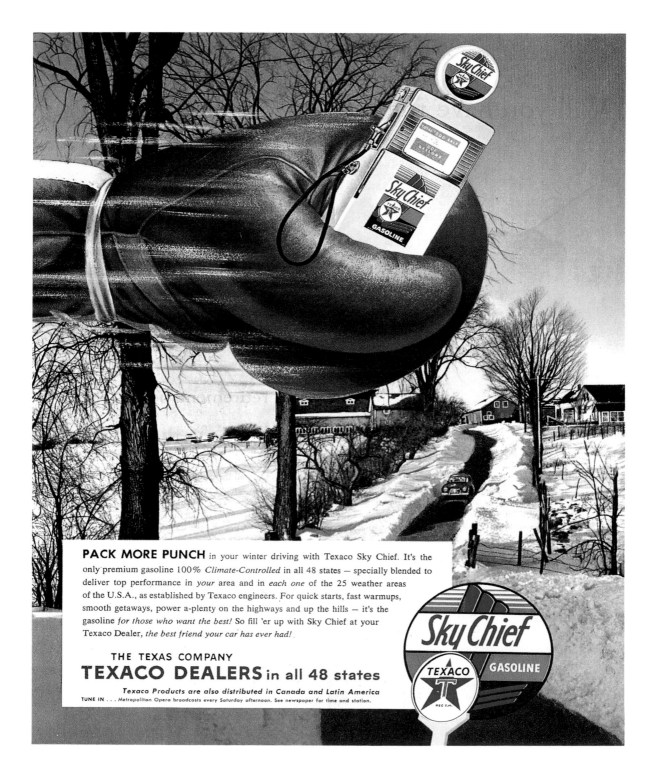

PACK MORE PUNCH in your winter driving with Texaco Sky Chief. It's the only premium gasoline 100% *Climate-Controlled* in all 48 states — specially blended to deliver top performance in *your* area and in *each one* of the 25 weather areas of the U.S.A., as established by Texaco engineers. For quick starts, fast warmups, smooth getaways, power a-plenty on the highways and up the hills — it's the gasoline *for those who want the best!* So fill 'er up with Sky Chief at your Texaco Dealer, *the best friend your car has ever had!*

THE TEXAS COMPANY
TEXACO DEALERS in all 48 states

Texaco Products are also distributed in Canada and Latin America
TUNE IN . . . Metropolitan Opera broadcasts every Saturday afternoon. See newspaper for time and station.

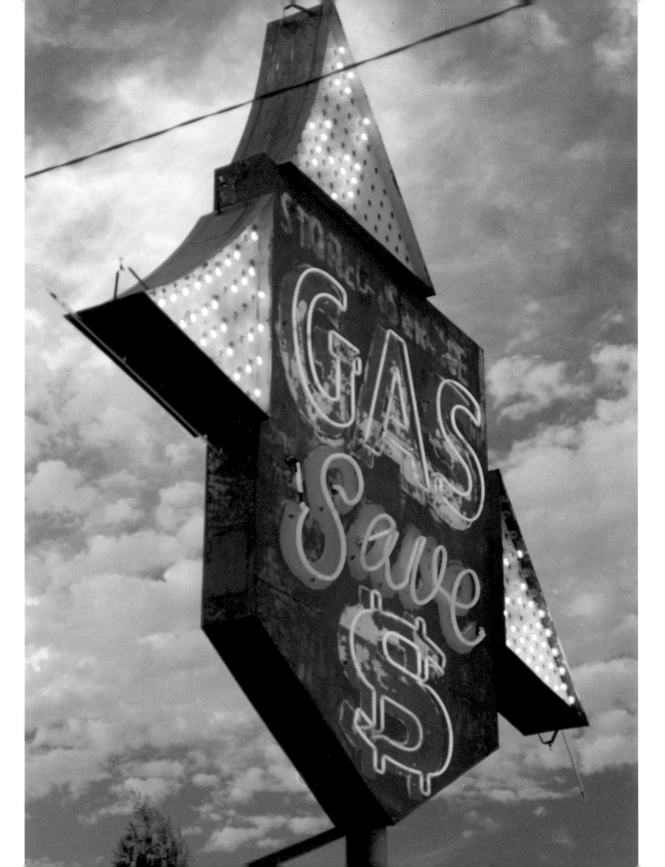

Chapter 6

SIGNS

During the dawn of America's automobile age, just hanging a hand-painted shingle by the roadside proved sufficient to peddle gas. With horse and buggy outnumbering the motorcar, the oil industry didn't require showy signs. Simple descriptions satisfied vehicle owners stranded because of an empty tank.

As the demand for gas increased and brands became important, refiners followed the lead of tobacco, soft-drink, and soap powder firms. By the turn of the century, their painted metal advertising signs already adorned a range of commercial structures—from corner grocer to ice-cream parlor. In rural towns and larger cities, businesses were covered in a patchwork quilt of incongruous advertising billboards.

While a majority of these "snipe" signs were simply painted tin, the most durable were made by fusing powdered glass onto metal sheeting with a high heat process. An extremely tough, "porcelain enameled" finish resulted, virtually impervious to wear and the destructive elements of nature. Featuring portability and ease of installation—they quickly became a hardy alternative to the

You Can Save Money Sign
Saving money has always been a major attraction for the motorist in need of a full tank of gasoline. In 1947, California independent dealer George Urich dreamed up a revolutionary new station concept targeted for California where customers could pump their own gas—pocketing the savings in the process. Initially opening three of his stations in the Los Angeles area, he forever altered the nature of the gasoline station and inadvertently set into motion a gasoline marketing controversy that would rage for years. Allowing customers to drive in and dispense fuel without the services of any sort of station attendant, Urich's new "Gas-A-Terias" consisted of eighteen to twenty-one gasoline pumps set on islands lined up at right angles to the street. Cars drove up to any one of these units in two long rows to refuel. Sometimes, patrons were parked twelve or fourteen abreast during peak periods! In the best cases, as little as two and a half minutes were required to pump gas, offering motorists the ability to refuel fast and get back on their way.

Standard Oval With Red Flame

Standard's "Torch and Oval" were once familiar players in the roadside movie. From the very early days of gas marketing until well into the mid-thirties, Standard stations were identified by either a Red Crown Gasoline sign or Polarine Motor Oil placard. From the early 1920s and on, a few of the company's products and some of the print advertising displayed the circular "Standard Oil Company Service" arrangement. This registered design incorporated a white torch with flame, positioned slightly offset over the letter "E" in "service." Around 1935, a rectangular identification sign was introduced by Standard—featuring the words "Standard Service" set within a colored field, surrounded by a thick rule. The familiar torch and oval design was adopted before the winter of 1945, although its physical implementation was hindered by post-war shortages. Fortunately, the delay proved cost-saving: before new signs could be installed, the white torch was upgraded to show off a blazing red flame. By 1948, the Standard Oil torch and flame were in full use, completely replacing the colorless version on all but product cans (they were revised in 1950).

Chevrolet Phillips 66 Sign

When the Phillips Petroleum Company introduced their new "66" gasoline during the late twenties, they didn't waste any time promoting their new product. As daring skywriters blazed across the wide blue yonder spreading the tradename of the new gasoline, company vehicles aided the public's familiarization with trunk mounted highway signs. Enlarged replicas of the familiar markers posted along Route 66, these over-sized signboards featured numerals outlined with light-catching "reflector buttons" (for maximum visability). When a car following turned on its head lamps, a moving reminder of Phillips' new motor fuel blazed a trail down the highway. *Courtesy Corporate Archives, Phillips Petroleum Company*

sign-painter's repertoire of cut pine and paint.

A perfect match for the grease and grime of the gas business, filling station operators soon contracted the services of sign makers

Flying Horse Stone With Sun
Pegasus ... Mobil's dauntless mascot—everywhere he's seen he commands attention. Striking a common chord in almost every motorist, he resonates feelings from deep within the imagination. In Greek mythology, Pegasus symbolized power and righteousness. When Perseus killed Medusa, Pegasus rose from the spilled blood. Residing in the house of the gods, he was the immortal royal steed who carried thunder and lightning for Zeus, king of the gods. For Socony (Standard Oil Company of New York) and later Mobil, the winged steed became the perfect choice to represent their products. During the '30s, renowned cowboy artist Robert Elmer took the original horse depicted here (installed above the doorway, Augusta Mobil Refinery bath house building, prior to 1993 demolition) and re-stylized it into the highly recognizable logo we know today as the "Flying Red Horse." For decades, it has been a familiar brush-stroke on the roadside canvas.
White Eagle Antique Mall Collection

and installed their own placards. Circular panels brandishing trademarks, corporate mascots, and a myriad of related pictures were proudly suspended from tall, slender poles planted close to the roadbed.

Eventually, portable versions made with supports of cast-iron were positioned in the direct line-of-sight of approaching vehicles. Often emblazoned with the likeness of a Gargoyle, Lion, or other mythical creature—matching discs of considerable diameter were installed at a place of prominence near the gable of the station structure.

To strengthen brand recognition and unify overall appearance, small reproductions of

Flying Horse on Fence Going Left

Billie Butler really loves red horses. She has a small herd corralled out in her backyard and a few of them tied up in the living room. Some of them are quite large, while others are small enough to occupy a place of prominence on top of a cabinet in her dining area. Two of her special favorites stand watch twenty-four hours per day just behind the television screen in her den. One poses on the corner of her tiny office desk. To the uninitiated, it might seem as if Mrs. Butler is in violation of local zoning ordinances and livestock laws.

But that couldn't be further from the truth! Her horses never need to be watered or curried—and mucking out a stable has never been one of her chores. For her, it's all perfectly natural. After all, the horses that share her small suburban home in Augusta, Kansas, are simply a collection of signs, statues, and plaques once used as advertising for the Mobil Oil Corporation. Butler started collecting the Flying Red Horse memorabilia years ago and has grown to love the striking symbol of speed and power. "Peggy" is definitely a part of her extended family. *Billie Butler Collection*

Neon Pegasus

A two-sided neon Pegasus flies above Gordon W. Smith's Mobil station in Eden Prairie, Minnesota. Smith's station was recently remodeled and lost all vestiges of its old, classic look—but the owner vowed to keep the sign as a neon crown atop his station. This is one of the last original neon Flying Horses in service in the United States. Pegasus was adopted as a trademark in the United States shortly after the organization of Socony-Vacuum in 1931, although the symbol was used as long ago as 1911. *Michael Dregni*

DX Neon Sign in Crate

The Mid-Continent Petroleum Company of Tulsa, Oklahoma, introduced their super-premium Diamond D-X brand of gasoline in the early thirties. Most of the company station outlets were rebranded with the Diamond D-X trademark by 1940. Eventually, the "Diamond" nomenclature was dropped and the D-X pair ruled station signs exclusively. Neon beauties like this red diamond sign soon lit up the roadways with their wonderful glow. Unfortunately, D-X moved towards a merger with the Sunray Oil Company in the mid-fifties, beginning the eventual demise of the geometric company symbol. In the regions where Sunoco gasoline was already being sold, the D-X name was phased out. Another gasoline brand name faded into obscurity, a hapless casualty of calculated business decisions.

these signs were permanently attached to fuel dispensers and other related service station equipment. Everywhere car customers fixed their gaze, clever phrases and flashy imagery hawked refined products. In a few years, the porcelain enameled sign became as ubiquitous as the gasoline pump.

As two-lane ribbons of asphalt became the new main streets for America, the motorist's attention span dwindled. While the pace of modern life quickened, the unpretentious advertising techniques of yesteryear began to show signs of age. Porcelain enameled signs were drained of their power to attract. The lifeless, one-dimensional placard had become commonplace—and was ultimately , taken for granted.

Fortunately, a radical advancement in sign technology caught the attention of ad executives: neon. Developed in Paris by the Claude Neon factory, Los Angeles car dealer Earle Anthony installed America's first neon sign in 1923. Outlined with clear blue tubing, his orange-red Packard show-stopper had a proven ability to slow traffic.

Soon, electrified "neon" gas illuminated signs at the service station. Shell outlined their golden seashell in yellow strips of light as Phillips 66 erected a colossal assembly of red tubing near Chicago's skyline. Socony's Flying Red Horse came to life in a blaze of glory, searing across the sky and onto the facade of the gasoline station. Petroleum companies had a new ally.

Since those unsophisticated days of horse, buggy, and hand-painted board, America's refueling outposts had, indeed, come a long, long way.

BEAR
WHEEL ALINEMENT
BALANCING
FRAME - AXLE
SERVICE

Pyro Anti-Freeze Thermometer

At one dollar per gallon, Super Pyro Anti-Freeze was one of the popular coolants available during the '30s and '40s. When Studebaker, Auburn, and DeSoto were still familiar names on the street, the ability to inhibit so-called "boil-away" at normal engine heat was an important feature. Taking its name from the Greek "Pyros," meaning heat or fire, Super-Pyro was an extremely appropriate name for an engine anti-freeze solution. For years, it was advertised with porcelain enameled signs of the variety shown here, along with another version depicting an engaging little snowman as product mascot. Still, the product moniker could not endure the test of time and eventually lost its visibility in the automotive market. As the unusual mania for starting fires became more widely recognized by its name (pyromania), a seemingly perfect brand image attained unfavorable connotations ... through no fault of its own.

Bear Service Alinement

Although not directly related to the petroleum business, yellow Bear Service signs were often (and can still be) seen attached to the wall at the corner gasoline service station. As part of the friendly pack of animals watching over the motorist, the laughing bear was always a welcome sight when the family sedan's steering wheel started to vibrate. Among the pack of wild creatures chosen to represent automotive and petroleum products, the bear takes honors as being the most common. One of the most visible examples of the bear motif was employed by California Standard: Adorning signs and other forms of advertising, their "Zerolene" polar bear poised precariously on an ice floe. Gas brands also incorporated the hibernating mammal to promote sales, capturing the motorist's imagination with brand names like "Grizzly" and "Polar." During the early '20s, the Bruin Oil and Refining Company marketed products with colorful pump globes featuring "The Bear of Them All" painted on curved glass. Continuing the trend during the '30s with their "Little Bear Gasoline," the Little Bear Oil and Refining Company ensured that the bear (as a widely used petroleum product symbol) survived for yet another generation.

SMOKE MEANS TROUBLE!

You NEEDN'T tell Johnny that smoke means trouble. He knows; he's learned the hard way.

And smoke from the exhaust of your car can mean plenty of trouble, too. For smoke usually comes from excessive engine wear—wear that wastes gas and oil—wear that only costly repairs can correct.

So every time you see smoke from the exhaust of a car, let it remind you of this:

Don't wait till it's too late! Change to Insulated Havoline Motor Oil NOW—and prevent needless wear that can make your car a "smoker."

Insulated Havoline is *insulated* to stand up to high engine heats that break down ordinary oils. Free-flowing when it is cold,

Insulated Havoline prevents those dry starts which are so wearing on cylinders and pistons.

And Insulated Havoline is also distilled to remove harmful, carbon-forming impurities. Change now to Insulated Havoline. At Texaco and other good dealers everywhere.

TUNE IN FRED ALLEN—Texaco Dealers invite you to enjoy Fred Allen in the full-hour program of the TEXACO STAR THEATRE...with Kenny Baker, Al Goodman's Orchestra and a great cast. Every Wednesday Night, Columbia Network. 9:00 E.S.T., 8:00 C.S.T., 10:00 M.S.T., 9:00 P.S.T.

DISTILLED AND INSULATED

...AGAINST HEAT...AGAINST COLD

TEXACO

HAVOLINE MOTOR OIL

DON'T WAIT UNTIL IT'S TOO LATE!

Your car was never designed to "smoke." Help reduce excessive wear in *your* motor before you join America's caravan of more than 3,000,000 "smokers." Prevent smoke that results from wear by using Insulated Havoline Motor Oil.

Chapter 7

SMOKING

When automobile refueling depots were first established along the roadways of early America, an open flame was considered highly dangerous. Because gasoline was routinely spilled during the crude fillup process, fumes often posed a serious safety risk for the beginning motorist.

During the early 1900s, the routine use of above ground storage tanks only increased the hazard. Arriving automobiles often passed within a few feet of the elevated reservoirs, causing endless worry for depot operators. Any manner of spark carelessly introduced within the reach of these vapors could prove explosive—and ultimately fatal.

Later, the widespread use of curbside pumping equipment and the addition of the filling hose shifted the dangers. The ritual of refueling an automobile moved from the sparsely populated outskirts of town to the higher density of the inner city.

By then, safety levels were increased only marginally. The introduction of underground holding tanks was a welcome improvement, but technical enhancements designed to protect against the fire threat demanded refinement.

While the introduction of the visible register gasoline pump promised a new lev-

Smoke Means Trouble
At the American service station, smoke meant trouble in more ways than one! According to early Texaco ads for their distilled and insulated Havoline Oil, automobiles were never "designed to smoke." Excessive motor wear caused by inferior lubrication products was the usual culprit behind sick vehicles, easily avoided by filling the crankcase with the right kind of motor oil. Discouraging little Johnny from experimenting with tobacco products was not quite so easy—but, provided the perfect advertising association to remind the motorist of what an engine might feel like if infiltrated with too much smoke. Still, in an age when oil companies were distributing matchbooks imprinted with their own advertising, it seems curious that a magazine ad would depict fire sticks in such a negative setting. *Courtesy Texaco Inc.*

Rolex Esso Lighter

Walking Billboard, Inc. of Chicago was one of the most visible manufacturers of cigarette lighter advertising pieces. By imprinting brand names and slogans on small, personal objects, their aim was to promote the sale of goods and services in ways conventional advertising could not. While a large sign lit with bright chase lights was a highly visible way to sell, it was too large to fit inside a purse or pocket. As portable ads, quality lighters (similar to this Rolex model) fit the bill. Ever since the dissolution of the Standard Oil Trust in 1911, legal restrictions have halted any company from using the Standard name (or the Esso derivative) on a national basis. As a result, the Esso brand introduced in 1926 was used in the East, Humble in Ohio, and Enco in other regions. Unfortunately, this made it difficult for Standard to achieve name recognition nationally. During the early '70s, the decision makers at Esso decided that a name change was in order—dubbing the top-secret project Operation Nugget. To guarantee security, top level executives typed their own memos and letters. The Enco name was considered, but quickly eliminated after further study (it meant "stalled car" in Japanese). Thousands of possibilities were investigated and a computer was employed to generate a list of meaningless letter combinations. After testing some of the final names in fifty-five languages and interviewing over 7,000 customers, the new identity was finally selected. A computer creation tailor-made for worldwide use was the winner: Exxon (the double "x" occurred only in the Maltese language)! Estimated cost for the entire name change project: $100 million. *Gyvel Young-Witzel Collection*

Skelly Matches and Book

The Skelly Oil Company decided to move against the popular norm by distributing stick matches (packaged within an under scale replica of a one-quart oil container) to its gasoline customers. Unlike most ordinary paper matches, these gold-tipped beauties left a most memorable impression with the discerning gasoline customer. To this end, the bold Skelly insignia and corporate colors played a large role in their external packaging. By today's safety standards, it's hard to believe that incendiary sticks like this were ever distributed by gasoline businesses. When burned, wooden match sticks of this type have a tendency to remain hot—even moments after their flame burns out. Consider the possibilities: If carelessly tossed out of a car window within the vicinity of gas pump's vapors or flicked into a rubbish bin near the oil can rack—a smoldering match stick could easily turn a refueling stop into a disaster area. *White Eagle Antique Mall Collection*

Phillips Cigarette Lighter
As an attention-getting alternative to paper matchbooks imprinted with advertising, refiners like the Phillips Petroleum Company joined other companies by distributing fancy cigarette lighters decorated with their corporate colors and trademark. Unlike the plastic throw-away versions offered for sale at the cash registers of today's mini-markets, these distinctive flame throwers were substantial units—proudly displayed and coveted by all of the smokers lucky enough to own one. As inhabitants of today's "throw-away" society, it's sometimes hard to imagine that only a few decades ago, ordinary sundries like the fountain pen, cigarette lighter, drinking cup, soft-drink bottle, and razor were used repeatedly—until they became completely unusable and needed permanent replacement. As more and more of our natural resources become depleted, the reusable attitudes of a previous generation are being rediscovered.

el of honesty, the mechanism employed to terminate fuel flow remained impractical. The standard gas pump filler hose still did not feature any type of hand-actuated flow valve at the end. A valve mounted on the pump unit controlled fluid release.

Motorists routinely miscalculated their tank's holding capacity, often resulting in excess gasoline spillage. For those fearless enough to indulge in the habit of smoking a cigar while topping off, the end was literally close at hand.

Fortunately, petroleum refiners began regulating these unsupervised procedures. Station equipment eventually became off-limits to motorists as full-time pump attendants shouldered the responsibility for refilling gas tanks. Signs were posted near pumps to warn against smoking and customers routinely instructed to kill their engines before service. Experienced servicemen ensured that all manner of flame was extinguished and that proper safety precautions were followed. Careless customers driving in with lit cigarettes dangling from their lips were immediately warned to extinguish them.

To re-ignite their stogies, smokers often visited the local drugstore and utilized the free gas flame provided at the cigar counter. Eventually, gasoline pump operators working along Main Street took notice. Those with foresight immediately recognized a new avenue for promoting their services.

Bowing to increased pressure from the matchbook salesmen, independent stations

Standard Ashtray with Patches
For the road traveler enamored of souvenirs from a trip, the basic ashtray has always proven itself quite popular. Major and minor tourist attractions sold (and still sell) them in large quantities along virtually every roadway in the country. Of course, a few business establishments serving the motorist use them purely for the purpose they were intended: to catch ashes falling from a lit cigarette and to hold their smoldering remains. Regardless of their use, one fundamental question has been endlessly debated by travelers down through the years: if an ashtray depicting advertising (text and images) is "appropriated" from a roadside business such as a hotel, restaurant, or gas station—is it theft? Aren't these glass receptacles placed there for the sole purpose of advertising? While the answer to this weighty question may never be found, the fact remains that the ashtray is the perfect, portable memento of long-distance road excursions.
Steve Perrault Collection

soon signed orders for books printed with their name and location. Major petroleum refiners followed. Eventually company stations and local operators all over the country were freely distributing the very means to their destruction.

In what seemed like a curious marriage, the gasoline refueling station and the matchbook became partners. The most feared enemy of the gasoline proprietor was now an important part of the overall advertising scheme.

Soon advertising by way of matchbook was regarded as a viable portion of the typical station's marketing. Not only were these minuscule billboards practical, they proved an economical way to promote gas brands. A colorful advertisement provided an instant reminder of where to refuel every time the motorist went to light up a cigarette.

Shur-Stop Fire Grenades

During the 1930s, a number of American chemical manufacturers produced some extremely physical examples of commercial fire fighting equipment. Companies like the Red Comet Company, Red Ball, and the International Fire Equipment Company manufactured and marketed sealed glass "grenades," filled with crimson-colored carbon tetrachloride. Usually, six of these chemical grenades were packed within a portable case, similar to this Shur-Stop kit. When a fire broke out at the gas station, restaurant, or factory, these hand-held crucibles were thrown into the flames by the nearest bystander. When the glass broke, the carbon-tetrachloride quickly inhibited further combustion. Although quite effective in some situations, they could be totally useless against combustion already firmly established. Most of the fire grenades were of the throw type, while some featured built-in pot metal with a heat-activated spring and plunger device. Offered in a wide assortment of decorative glass and fancy holders, some were suspended from the ceiling or attached to the wall. When external heat reached a certain temperature, fluid would automatically spray onto the fire. Utilized widely at various commercial enterprises (including gasoline stations), carbon-tetrachloride grenades enjoyed a short-lived popularity before the advent of the more practical, and highly effective, dry-chemical extinguishers in use today. *Frank J. Liska Collection*

Opposite

Buddy, Can You Spare a Light?

Today, gasoline station advertising matchbooks exist as miniature windows into America's gas station glory days. Rife with the potent imagery of customer service, quality, unbridled speed, everlasting power, and convenience—they are clear evidence of this nation's love affair with the automobile. Despite warnings from the Surgeon General, the relationship between cigarettes, the American highway, and the gasoline service station remains as strong as it ever was. To the chagrin of the modern motorist in search of scenery, an endless procession of billboards hawk almost every brand of smoke—along virtually every mile of roadway. To augment these roadside messages, matchbooks continue to be passed out freely—the innocent themes popularized by yesteryear's gas businesses superseded by the cool attitudes of Joe Camel. Gone are the naive depictions of station attendants and carefree couples out for a Sunday drive. *Michael Witzel © 1993, Matchbooks from Steve Perrault Collection*

STANDARD

TOUR

CONOCO
TRAVEL
BUREAU
CONTINENTAL
OIL COMPANY
DENVER
COLORADO

TRADE MARK

Prepa

Especi

Quality Products
WENDELL WENTLING
Phone CO 8-2165 or CO 8-3584
BEAVER CITY, NEBR.

CEN

Chapter 8

PREMIUMS

In 1914, the mortar on Gulf's first Pennsylvania service station wasn't even dry when advertising man William Akin suggested the company mail road maps of Allegheny County to all of its registered motorists.

Ten-thousand guides were delivered without charge, resulting in a pleasant surprise for many local car owners. Since existing roadways were poorly marked and written directions cumbersome, road maps were regarded as a practical and useful gift.

Many delighted recipients responded with their cars at the pumps. Business boomed and station attendants began handing out even more road maps. Soon, guides featuring the surrounding states were printed as new customers associated generosity with the "Sign of the Orange Disk."

Other oil concerns quickly followed Gulf's lead. By the mid-twenties, virtually every major refiner offered maps—and other free goods to their customers. Products were now a major part of the promotional equation, including license plate emblems, paper radiator shields, glassware, fountain

Standard Oil Sign Thermometer
When all of the petroliana (gas and oil collectibles) currently available have been collected, what will be left for future treasure hunters? Are some of the gasoline advertising and promotional goods being distributed by today's quickie marts worth stashing away for a future collection? Will sports bottles, drink cups, and other ordinarily mundane retail items become the gas station heirlooms of tomorrow? Could a plastic Früsen Gladjen container someday be worth something? It's anyone's guess. After all, who could have predicted thirty years ago that a Standard Oil sign made into a miniature plastic thermometer would someday be worth a twenty dollar bill? No one can accurately gauge the possible worth of any object in the future, much less make a more than educated guess at what kind of item that might be. What about Batman memorabilia, pizza delivery boxes, gum wrappers, Star Wars toys, and trash can liners: tomorrow's treasures? Stick around a few more decades, only then will we know for sure!
White Eagle Antique Mall Collection

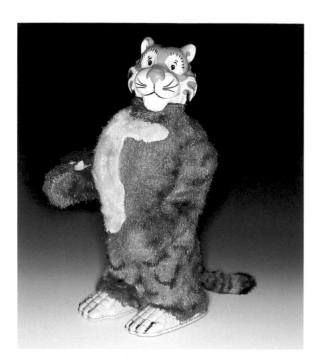

Put a Tiger in Your Tank Toy

"Put a Tiger in Your Tank" was one of the gasoline industry's most memorable slogans. For Esso (changed to Exxon in 1972), the dynamic orange feline was the perfect match for Mobil's Flying Red Horse. Like Pegasus, the black-striped mascot symbolized speed, agility, and power—a potent combination to represent gasoline and automotive products. But that's where the similarities between the Tiger and the Flying Red Horse ended: pleased with the positive effect of their down-to-earth trademark, Standard Oil of New Jersey (Esso) released a number of station premiums and promotional toys in support of the striped beast. Along with the usual key-chains and knick-knacks, a fur covered tiger with wind-up motor shuffled into the hearts and minds of young and old service station visitors. Factoid: Many of the old-time executives from the Powerine Company (bought out by Standard Oil of New Jersey) attest to the fact that their original tiger trademark inspired the entire Esso campaign. Reportedly, the advertising idea was developed in Europe first, where the feline was reworked into a cartoon format. Soon after the promotional campaign became a proven winner overseas, the concept was brought back to the states and introduced to American gasoline consumers. *White Eagle Antique Mall Collection*

White Eagle
Balanced Ethyl
Gasoline
and
Keynoil
The Original
High Compression Motor Oil

Free Air and Water, Reliable Road Information
Clean Rest Rooms—To Enjoy Your Trip

White Eagle Balanced Gasoline and Keynoil

Official 1929

MOTOR TRAILS MAP
OF
Western Missouri KANSAS Eastern Colorado

White Eagle
Balanced Ethyl
Gasoline
and
Keynoil
The Original
High Compression Motor Oil

Previous page
White Eagle Station With Autos
During the twenties and thirties, the automobile road maps and travel guides passed out free of charge to customers were often colorful showcases for all manner of art. Scenes rife with motor vehicles, aircraft, station attendants, gasoline pumps, trademark signs, bucolic landscapes, and cars full of passengers made it onto the tri-fold covers of these handy commercial booklets. The adventurous fun and whimsy of motoring over America's roadways became their dominant theme, combined with the boundless good nature of the neighborhood service station operator and his pumping staff. While the oil company road map may have been a useful tool, it served a greater purpose: popularizing the notion of motor travel for pleasure, vacations taken by car ... and the unbridled consumption of gallons of gasoline.
White Eagle Antique Mall Collection

Shell's Anti-Screwdriver Crusade
During the latter part of the thirties, Shell Oil Company service stations became headquarters for a nationwide Share-the-Road Crusade. According to traffic authorities, twenty-five percent of all Stop-and-Go was caused by thoughtless, selfish drivers—by "Screwdrivers." When motorists drove into the local "Show your colors" Shell station, they would receive a free booklet that illustrated these careless driving mistakes and how to improve them. In addition, a friendly service station attendant would attach a free Share-The-Road emblem to the customer's automobile license plate. Not only would the colorful insignia and colored flags inform others that you were doing your part to eliminate careless driving, it sold gasoline, too. As the booklet stated: "For the Stop-and-Go driving that can't be avoided, we recommend Super-Shell. With Super-Shell and 'Share-the-Road,' everybody saves!" *Courtesy Shell Oil Company*

pens, toys, matches, lens-tissue, fans, ink-blotters, hand-lotion, and even replica service stations.

While air for the tires and water for the radiator were recognized as helpful service station amenities, they lacked the pizzazz required to capture the imagination of the modern vehicle owner. Filling stations that distributed entertaining trinkets and automotive accessories were remembered. Gifts showered upon the wife and children commanded lasting attention—the kind that cemented true brand loyalty miles on down the highway.

Some giveaways were in exchange for repeated patronage, others simply for driving in to have the oil checked. Many premiums related directly to the gasoline or lubricant marketed, while others bore no association at all. The complimentary gift was often not as important as its intended message: This service station establishment and parent company care enough about the customer to give him more than he bargained for.

Historically, the majority of these petroleum giveaways functioned purely as vehicles for advertising. Highly visible, the phone number and address of the participating gasoline dealer almost always appeared somewhere on the gratis object. Paper-based merchandise such as hand-held fans, children's games, and small thermometers provided the perfect medium for printed promotions.

In many cases, the complimentary goods bore only the trademark of the parent company or insignia of a particular gasoline brand. Sometimes, objects themselves were modeled after a real-life piece of

WITH THIS EMBLEM—SHOW YOUR COLORS!

Join this crusade against "SCREWDRIVERS"
-help cut STOP-and-GO 25%

WE Shell dealers have started something! In addition to selling Super-Shell, the gasoline which cuts the *cost* of Stop-and-Go, we're headquarters for the nation-wide Share-the-Road crusade to cut the *amount* of Stop-and-Go!

Traffic authorities say 25% of all Stop-and-Go is caused by thoughtless, selfish driving—by "Screwdrivers."

The *Share-the-Road* Club is out to correct this condition. Public opinion can curb "Screwdrivers"—cut Stop-and-Go 25% right now!

SHOW YOUR COLORS—come in and we'll attach the Shell Share-the-Road emblem to your car FREE. We'll give you a booklet that shows the boners "Screwdrivers" pull.

For the Stop-and-Go driving that *can't* be avoided, we recommend Super-Shell. With Super-Shell and "Share the Road," *everybody* saves!

WIDE-MODEL "SCREWDRIVER" — 20 miles an hour is his pace—but you need an airplane to pass him! A line of cars jams up behind, and needless Stop-and-Go results . . . Remember, your engine uses 3 *times* as much gasoline in low and second gears as in high—when a "Screwdriver" forces you to shift gears, *you pay!*

"Share the Road" and SUPER-SHELL both save on STOP-and-GO

service station equipment. Many premiums were reproductions of corporate mascots, intended for permanent display on the family flivver.

Like the prize at the bottom of the Cracker-Jack box, the gas station premium was that little extra value we motorists looked forward to when purchasing our gasoline. Whether a coin bank fashioned in the form of a diminutive oil can or pair of petite gasoline pumps intended for salt and pepper, their prime intention was to remind us where the most generous gasoline dealer on the boulevard could be found.

A tiny uniformed Esso man or transistor radio disguised as a car battery might not have been something we really needed, but it sure was fun when it was handed to us... for free.

Pegasus License Placard Route 66

Mobil's license plate ornament embossed with the Flying Red Horse mascot is one of the genre's most graphic. A number of different versions were manufactured, including types to promote safe driving, patriotism, and even the California World's Fair. From today's perspective, these engaging placards illustrate just how radically different automotive designs were during the years when bumpers were made of metal and dashboards trimmed in wood. It used to be that the tail end of an automobile protruded far from the rear of the chassis. Trunks were often enormous affairs, usually large enough to hold the luggage for an entire family. The area for license plate mounting was an uncomplicated affair, with plenty of extra clearance available to attach any number of placards handed out by businesses. Unfortunately, new body styling and the radical redesign of bumpers caused the prominence of the license plate mounting area to wane, rendering these colorful advertising placards obsolete.

Mobilgas Salt & Pepper

During the age of limitless service station premiums, Salt & Pepper shakers were manufactured by novelty companies for the major refiners. Inexpensively molded from plastic, these branded giveaways proved a practical and economical method to increase patronage. With their compact design, they provided the retailer with a clever means by which to infiltrate the suburban home. An endless supply of these inexpensive spice dispensers were routinely distributed to regular customers—eventually finding their place on top of dinette tables. Once firmly established and accepted as another household object, the unassuming shakers would work their magic. When breakfast, lunch, or dinner called for additional flavor, the oil refiner's trademark was there—ready to serve. Later, when a dipping fuel gauge called for gas, the subconscious did the rest. Tasty memories became the gas station's asset. *Gary Rawlings Collection*

HEY, KIDS!

It's simple to own one of the keen scale model Mobilgas Tank Trucks illustrated on this card.

Because we are anxious to meet you and your folks and acquaint them with our brand of service, we are offering you a free scale model Mobilgas Tank Truck.

Just get Mom or Dad to drive into our station today and fill up with Mobilgas "R" or Mobilgas Special. Every time they purchase 5 gallons we will mark off one of the 5-gallon squares shown on purchase card in upper right-hand corner.

When all squares shown on this card have been marked off by us (representing purchase of 40 gallons) this scale model Mobilgas Tank Truck will be *yours* absolutely free.

So get started on your fleet of trucks today. Ask the folks to drive in and fill up with Mobilgas. There's no limit to the number of these trucks you can own. We have them in stock now! — See you soon!

Actual Photo of Mobilgas model Tank Truck

Mobilgas Red Oil Tanker on Wood

Mobilgas service stations rewarded loyal customers with scale replicas of company tank trucks (like this tin example) at most of their retail outlets during the forties and fifties. For the lucky baby-boomer riding shotgun, anticipating the next filling station prize was a thought eclipsed only by the images of cheeseburgers and ice cream cones. To pass the time while motoring down one of America's limitless highways—there was nothing like having a brand new service station premium to play with. "Ask the folks to drive in and fill up with Mobilgas, there's no limit to the number of these trucks you can own. We have them in stock now—see you soon!" *Billie Butler Collection*

186

Mobilgas Truck Card

When parents couldn't be convinced to visit the local service station, youngsters were often employed to coax their elders in for other purposes. Premium offers like this Mobilgas tank truck promotion were a successful way for refiners to increase patronage and ensure repeat business. Once the parent/vehicle owner pumped his or her first five gallons of gasoline, they were effectively hooked! From then on, the copilot in the back seat would take hold of the purchase card and begin to dream—bound and determined to remind the one behind the wheel where to refuel once the gas gauge dipped into the empty zone. *Red Horse Museum Collection*

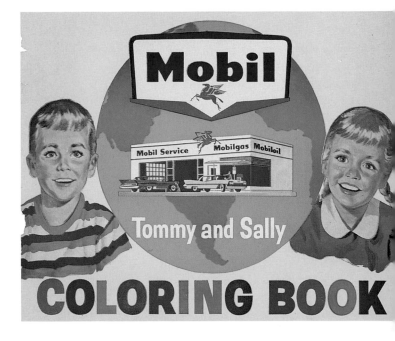

Plastic Shell Truck

Everyone knows that toy cars and trucks rank extremely high in the pecking order of children's favorite toys. The desire for a new model or type can be so strong for a small child that he or she would do anything to persuade his or her parents to visit the toy store or business where they might be purchased. Service stations were in tune to this fact early on and began to offer colorful tin-trucks as attractive incentive items. Some were given away with no strings attached at special grand-openings and promotions, while others required parents to fill up with a pre-determined amount of gasoline before a punch card could be redeemed for the multi-wheeled prize. Shell, Mobil, Gulf, Sinclair, and a host of other oil refiners offered a wide variety of these toy gasoline tankers. Yet, unlike some of the other features of the American gas station that have fallen by the wayside, the concept of the scaled-down gasoline tanker still lives. Texaco promotes a new model every year, much to the delight of today's generation of young truckers. *White Eagle Antique Mall Collection*

Tommy and Sally Coloring Book

To capture the attention of the automobile's youthful passengers, petroleum refining companies like Mobil Oil printed coloring books to be passed out as promotional give-aways. Inside, outlined pictures depicted the various ways company products were refined, marketed, and ultimately used. With crayons, children would fill in the colors of a service attendant's uniform, station buildings, and refining facilities—in effect, producing their own paper advertising materials. Sure to remind them of their favorite gas station once they reached driver's license age, the coloring book was a clever medium for training future generations of automobile owners where to go for service, value, and quality.

Phillips 66 Give-Away Montage

Phillips Petroleum was one of many gasoline refiners that offered premium gifts to everyday customers. When the time came to refill the gas tank, a friendly station attendant could always be counted on for another interesting trinket. Young and old alike looked forward to their next service station visit, eager to receive the goodies produced from the pockets of the pump operators. Small souvenirs such as key-chains, plastic letter openers, and ice-scrapers could be manufactured economically in large quantities—making them a perfect choice for gratis distribution. Of course, the imprinted brand name and station location played a large role in the effectiveness of these baubles. Free premium goods were (and still are) a potent form of good will advertising, free from the annoying repetitiveness of jingles and overly familiar slogans. *Red Horse Museum Collection*

Texaco Fire-Chief Toy Hat

In an attempt to offset the economic effects of the "great" depression, Texaco introduced its Fire-Chief Gasoline in 1932. To inaugurate the new addition, comedian Ed Wynne (known over the airwaves as the "Perfect Fool") kicked off a full-scale comedy radio program—broadcast from coast-to-coast on the NBC network. As the first large-scale radio show to raise a glass curtain between the audience and performers (and broadcast live), the Texaco Fire-Chief show proved to be an effective promotional vehicle for the company's new automotive gasoline. To heighten the public's awareness of the new motor fuel and to further exploit the "fire" theme, Texaco later offered plastic firefighter hats at dealer outlets. Boxed with the familiar "You can trust your car to the man who wears the star" slogan emblazoned on cardboard, they quickly became the ultimate delight for many youngsters. With a battery powered microphone and small loudspeaker embedded into the helmet front, they provided the imaginative firefighter-to-be hours of fun. *White Eagle Antique Mall Collection*

Phillips 66 Banks and Rain Gauge

Along with rain gauges and other sundry gadgets, personal coin banks became a popular give-away item for petroleum refiners. Most notably, the so-called "fatman" coin bank (made of plastic) became a favorite among gasoline marketers, many utilizing the rotund example shown in this lineup as a station premium. Complete with molded attendant's hat, standard uniform, black bow-tie, shined shoes, and beaming grin—these diminutive money receptacles consolidated all of the features of the station pump jockey into one portable package. Along with the circular style banks made in the miniaturized shape of a one-quart oil container, they became effective advertisements for all manner of product and services. Holding the customer's loose change constituted only a small part of their important job. *Red Horse Museum Collection*

S&H Green Stamp Booklet

Anyone who has ever eaten at a roadside hamburger stand with carhop service or chomped on popcorn at a drive-in movie theater knows what S&H Greenstamps are. At businesses all across America, proprietors once passed out these small green booklets to customers. Whenever a retail purchase was made at participating establishments, ribbons of perforated stamps were distributed—in direct proportion to the total cash amount of the customer's purchase. As stamps were accumulated, they were licked and pasted inside booklets, until all of the pages were filled. Completed booklets were traded for merchandise (toasters, lawn furniture, bicycles) at redemption centers located in various regions of the country. American consumers quickly took to this added incentive program and service stations eagerly embraced the clever rebate system. Established in 1896 by the Sperry and Hutchinson Company, Green Cooperative Cash Discount Stamps were once a familiar part of buying gasoline.

Flying Horse Key-Chain

A large majority of petroleum concerns passed out free key-chains as station premiums. Among the roster of products available, these diminutive freebies often provided the most cost-effective solution in the arena of complimentary incentive gifts. The key-chain was a perfect choice for promotion, too. It was easily carried, highly useful, and performed a very important task: keeping car keys organized and in one place. Some of the more useful versions incorporated plastic coin holders, nail clippers, and even pen-knives. One unusual model distributed by Socony and others featured a small tube with enough space inside to store a rolled-up driver's license or emergency cash! Not surprisingly, a few oil refiners went one step further than the basic key-chain by offering actual key blanks featuring their company logo. The automobile ignition key could now feature the owner's favorite brand! *Red Horse Museum Collection*

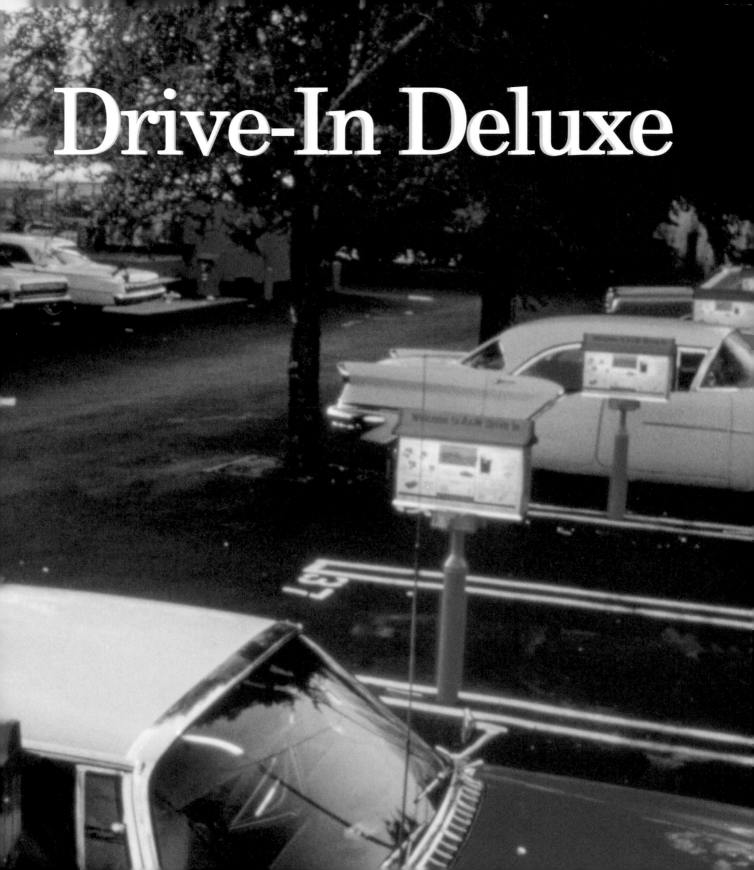

Drive-In Deluxe

Acknowledgments

A triple-thick thank you goes out to all the people who donated time, knowledge, recollections, photos, advertisements, contacts, and suggestions, most notably A & W Restaurants, Inc.; the Coca-Cola Company; Michael Dregni; the Dr. Pepper Museum of Waco, Texas; Albert Doumar; Ralph Grossman; Hanna-Barbera Entertainment Company; Ramona Longpre; Marriott Corporation; Richard McDonald; Clare Patterson; Louise Sivils; Sonic Industries, Inc.; Steak n' Shake, Inc.; Texas Pig Stands Inc.; Universal Studios Florida; Buna "Johnnie" Van Hekken; Steven Weiss; and June Wian. A steaming-hot pot of fresh coffee is reserved for the many archives, artists, and talented photographers that provided appropriate drive-in images, including Howard Ande, the Atlanta Historical Society, Kent Bash, Annabelle Breakey, the helpful and always knowledgeable staff at CoolStock, the great researchers at the Dallas Public Library, the Georgia Historical Society, Glen Icanberry, Brett Parker, Louis Persat, Preziosi Postcards, Quincy Historical Society, Jim Ross, the Security Pacific Historical Photograph Collection, Bob Sigmon, Andy Southard, Jr., Tombrock Corporation, University of Louisville Ekstrom Library, and Randy Welborn. Finally, a second helping of thanks is served to Joan Johnson of Circa Research and Reference, Douglas Photographic, and Imagers.

The author hanging out at Mel's Drive-In restaurant, seen here with the classic, yellow deuce coupe of *American Graffiti* movie fame and the 1950 custom Mercury "MRL MIST." The hot rod is now owned by car collector Rick Figari of San Francisco, California, and the lead sled by Marvin Giambastiani.
Annabelle Breakey

Introduction

WHAT IS A DRIVE-IN RESTAURANT?

According to strict definition, a drive-in restaurant is a specialized eating establishment that employs a staff of parking lot servers, or carhops, to deliver food and drinks to customers waiting in their cars. There, a small tray that holds the ordered items is clipped onto the window where it provides a miniature table for the dining visitor. As they eat, patrons may enjoy private conversation in the car, listen to the radio, or just sit back, relax, and watch the sights. At any time, they may make an additional order or request from the carhop on call. When their appetites are satiated, it's customary that they leave a small tip on the tray. When they are ready to leave, the tray is removed from the car, and they may pull out into traffic unhindered.

The term *drive-in* has grown to include a much wider range of roadside restaurants and now may be applied to dining spots that don't offer carhop service. But to gain admittance into the wayside fraternity of the traditional drive-in restaurant, there are a few rules that must be followed: First, the eatery must be visited primarily by patrons arriving by automobile, motorcycle, motor home, or other type of conveyance (food stands at the local mall are definitely out). The drive-in must serve up delicious, old-fashioned drinks, desserts, and road food and be free of all of the pomp and circumstance that's found at the more upscale sit-down restaurants. Most important, it must convey the ambiance so adored by car-food connoisseurs.

In the visual department, vintage architecture is a big plus, as is a prodigious amount of neon tubing, the availability of tabletop jukebox controls (with three plays for a quarter) in those establishments that offer indoor seating, and menus that are encased in thick plastic with those little metal tabs on the corners to protect them from wear and tear. The reticent waitress who's wearing a pair of those funny little cat's-eye glasses (preferably attached to a chain) and a classic pink uniform with her first name embroidered on the front pocket can often bring an ordinary greasy spoon into the hallowed category of the drive-in. It's sufficient to say that any eatery offering the slightest hint of nostalgia—and boasting a heritage in pop culture—fits into the category of "drive-in deluxe."

With this broader definition in mind, your nearest drive-in restaurant could very well be the gleaming stainless steel diner parked down the boulevard. At the same time, the funky little coffee shop that's located downtown—the one where everyone hangs out sipping coffee and smoking cigarettes—could be considered a drive-in as well. When the craving for creamy dessert foods arises, it's the walk-up dairy stand located on the outskirts of town that provides the drive-in satisfaction so many people are looking for. In that same vein, the myriad walk-up burger joints that cling to survival all across America are drive-ins in their own right, as are the tiny mom-and-pop taco shops, hot dog havens, burrito bars, and soft drink stands that make up that fast food underbelly of the culinary world. The American drive-in restaurant is a state of mind, a feeling that's waiting for us out there along the back roads of America, usually when we least expect it and our taste buds are ready for a roadside treat.

Chapter One

THE ORIGINS OF DRIVE-IN DINING

During the latter part of the 1800s, most of America's city pharmacies housed the bubbling apparatus used to produce carbonated water. In the sunny South, hot summer temperatures heated up the growing demand for syrup-flavored soda until it became one of the standard commodities of Main Street. By the turn of the century and the dawn of the motorcar, the obsession to consume soda water became the catalyst that forced conventional food and drink operations to consider new and improved ways of serving customers.

To satisfy the growing demand for those tasty soda-water treats that tickled the taste buds and soothed the palate, savvy merchandisers established a new precedent for public refreshment and diversion. Much like the ubiquitous fast food restaurants of the present day, a myriad of commercial enterprises sprang up along the urban

In the late part of the second decade, the Edgewood Pharmacy in Dallas, Texas, was typical of similar drugstore operations doing business. Runners were employed as waiters to the curbside, taking out to waiting cars refreshments that were previously available only to walk-in customers. The format was the predecessor to the drive-ins that emerged during the early 1920s. *Dallas Public Library*

The drive-in restaurant made its debut in the Hanna-Barbera television cartoon the *Flintstones*. Back in those prehistoric times, a big rack of ribs was a popular item, in spite of the fact that its sheer weight could tip over the vehicle. *Hanna-Barbera Productions, Inc. ©1996, All Rights Reserved. Turner Broadcasting Systems, Inc. ©1996, All Rights Reserved*

corridors in order to take advantage of the burgeoning trend. The city of Atlanta, Georgia, was a typical example of the increasing availability of fizzy liquid fun: By 1886, five fully equipped soda fountains were dispensing their sweet delights throughout the town and even more fountains were on the way!

As citizens made visiting the local pharmacy and its soda bar a recognized part of their daily rituals, the act of consuming nonalcoholic beverages simply for pleasure gained increased acceptance as a social activity. Arriving by foot, horse, or carriage—both men, women, and children regularly frequented the soda fountains in an effort to relax and escape their everyday woes. In an era that was devoid of radio, television, and other forms of popular entertainment, sipping a soda was found to be an excellent way to pass the time and to socialize with others (the future patrons of the drive-in eateries would mirror this same cultural activity).

At the turn of the century, the Coca-Cola Company promoted its syrup throughout the South with posters and point-of-purchase items that depicted people in their carriages being served by waiters. These runners were often employed by pharmacies to carry out refreshing beverages to people waiting in their horse-drawn coaches.
Courtesy Coca-Cola Company

As more and more pharmacies decided to add car service to their way of doing business, the moveable serving tray became a part of the everyday utensils used to serve the public. Trays attached to the window or door and featured some sort of bracket that braced against the body of the automobile.
Dallas Public Library

By the late 1920s, the Texas Pig Stands were moving away from their simple beginnings and began to try new forms of architecture for their drive-in units. This simple, octagonal concession design (constructed in the city of Los Angeles) was a precursor to the grand monuments that were erected by Harry Carpenter and Bill Simon during the 1930s. *Courtesy Texas Pig Stands, Inc.*

Crammed in among the pills and potions, the typical soda fountain serving arrangement included a large counter area or elaborate marble bar that functioned as a concession stand. Some establishments even provided areas where ornate tables and chairs were set up for more relaxed drinking. But as civilized as these conditions were, the growing penchant for consuming tasty drink invariably caused some problems. The menfolk, who had a nasty habit of chewing tobacco, smoking cigars, and engaging in bawdy conversation, often offended the more genteel female clientele. When the local soda fountains became overly crowded, sensibilities were assaulted.

The indignities weren't ignored for long and a number of solutions were examined. One of the most memorable accommodations to be made

The Texas Pig Stand operation is credited with being the first in America to implement the idea of a dedicated drive-in that serves food and drinks. Their present-day restaurant—one of many—still operates in San Antonio, Texas, and pays homage to the early years with this sign posted at the carhop lanes. *Michael Karl Witzel*

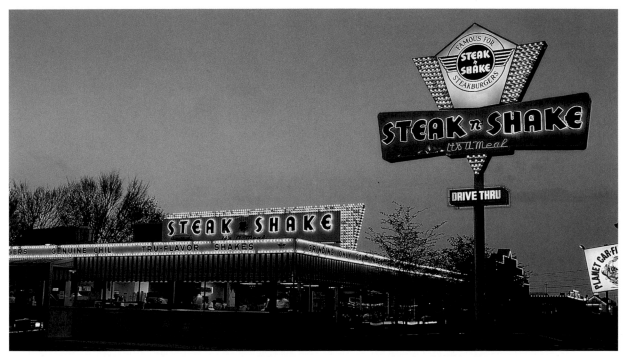

Steak n' Shake restaurants were started by Gus Belt back in 1934. He based the operation on a "Steakburger" that was made with finer cuts of ground beef and milkshakes that were hand-dipped with real ice cream. Although the carhops are ancient history, the outfit still thrives as a popular fast food chain throughout the midwestern regions of the United States. *Howard Ande*

for the express convenience of "mobile" customers gained notoriety in Memphis, Tennessee. It all started in 1905 when horse-drawn carriages were pulling up to Harold Fortune's drugstore carrying passengers eager to partake of the tasty potions sold inside. According to legend, the business was so brisk one summer evening that a local man came up with the revolutionary idea of allowing the ladies to wait in their carriages while he braved the crowds and made all the drink orders. He then hand-delivered the sarsaparilla and other concoctions to the women as they perched in their surreys.

Of course this gentlemanly style of outside service was received quite well by all who were there, and by the end of the summer, word of the incident had spread throughout the town. Sud-

denly, upscale patrons were driving by with their chauffeured carriages to take advantage of the new "service." Caught off guard, Mr. Fortune was forced to rely on the young lads who were already employed at his fountain as counter servers. Unfortunately, it was soon discovered that the new procedure took too much time away from the employee's normal activities. A staff of delivery boys was hired to assume the hurried task of delivering soda water to people queuing up out in the street.

The setup became so immensely popular that even the Coca-Cola Company, one of the leading producers of syrup for the fountains, adopted the idea of serving people in their carriages as the theme for one of their early print advertising campaigns. Posters showing fashion-

The Texas Pig Stands experimented with a number of building styles during the drive-in's formative years. One of their most unusual designs was a pig-shaped structure that operated in the south-central Texas area. Recently, the vintage stand was discovered and plans are currently in work to restore the structure and return it to its former glory. *Michael Karl Witzel*

The Pig n' Whistle was one of the classic roadside eateries that opened for business in the South. The chain began in California as a tearoom in 1910 and spread across the country until it stopped in Macon, Georgia. Drive-in service was added in the 1920s, and by the 1950s future celebrities such as Little Richard, Otis Redding, and James Brown worked there as carhops. A sandwich called the "Pig Special" once sold there for 20 cents. "That piping, dancing little Pig with the jolly, 'come hither' smile has all sorts of good things for your refreshment and entertainment. . . ." *Author collection*

PIG'N WHISTLE
"UP AND DOWN THE COAST"

BREAKFASTS
LUNCHEONS
DINNERS
PARTIES
BANQUETS
CANDIES
PASTRIES
SODAS
ICES

As the pharmacy gained notoriety as the place to hang out and take a cool soda refreshment, the lad working behind the counter attained a certain mystery and mystique about him. Known by the public as a "soda jerk," this nonalcoholic barkeep appeared in numerous movies and slowly worked his way into the popular culture of our nation. *CoolStock/Library of Congress photo*

able women drinking their refreshments in their carriages caught the public's eye and furthered the cause of curbside soda fountain service.

After the automobile gained a strong foothold in the domestic market, the imbibe-in-your-vehicle concept was taken to an entirely new level: revised ads portrayed a carload of revelers enjoying effervescent tumblers of Coca-Cola while seated in their motoring coach. If that wasn't convenient enough, additional point-of-purchase prints showcased waiters who delivered beverages out to trains, boats, and other modes of transportation.

By that time, Fortune had relocated his growing fountain operation to the busy business district of Memphis and was introducing neophyte motoring enthusiasts to the magic of car service. Business became so good that a rabble of overeager automobilists frequently jammed the streets in an effort to get a cool drink. A hasty plan was implemented that called for the curb to be taken out in front of the establishment so that the waiting vehicles could pull up more closely to the front of the building (and right up on the sidewalk). Unfortunately, the stop-gap measure failed to alleviate the car congestion.

The Memphis city fathers overreacted to the complaints of nearby businesses and enacted an ordinance that banned any sort of car-oriented curb service in the downtown business district. Once again, Fortune moved his outfit—this time to a remote location on the outskirts of the city where traffic control and the complaints of neighbors wouldn't be a problem. It was 1922 when he constructed a brand new store that featured an even larger, separate fountain operation, kitchen facilities, and an oversized parking lot area. At last, dozens of automobiles could pull right in, find a space, and take advantage of unhurried front-seat service.

Surprisingly, Fortune was not the first to open the nation's premiere dedicated drive-in restaurant. One year earlier, the visionary team of Dallas, Texas, candy and tobacco magnate Jessie G. Kirby and physician Reuben W. Jackson beat Fortune at the drive-in dining game by opening the first roadside eatery that was specifically earmarked to sell lunch, dinner, and bottled refreshments at the curb. Unlike Fortune's Memphis fountain operation and the dozens of other imitators who copied its success throughout the South, the Texas restaurant was designed and built from the ground up with its sole intention to serve modern motorists right in their cars. This devoted drive-in concept was the brainchild of Kirby who had a hunch that the habits of the lackadaisical vehicle owner could be readily converted into cold, hard cash. "People with cars are so lazy that they don't want to get out of them to eat!" was the creed that he uttered when he tried to convince Jackson, his future partner, to invest the capital Kirby needed to start up the nation's first drive-in sandwich business. Jackson was captivated by Kirby's dramatic sales pitch and provided the $10,000 financing needed to build the prototype restaurant stand that was geared specifically to serving patrons while they remained seated in their cars.

In the fall of 1921, two American icons—the roadside restaurant and the motorcar—gave birth to an entirely new form of dining, the drive-in restaurant. That year, Kirby and Jackson's ambitious eatery, dubbed the "Pig Stand," began selling its delicious fare of "Pig sandwiches" and soft drinks from a small shack on the busy Dallas-Fort Worth Highway. Kirby's initial hunch was correct, and before too long the Lone Star state was abuzz with complimentary news of the Pig Stand's friendly carhop service, great food, and superior convenience. The drive-in was king.

Thirty-four years later both Kirby and Jackson had passed on, but Pig Stands were going stronger than ever. Former carhop Royce Hailey took over the reins and led the eatery and the numerous duplicates that bore its name into the halcyon days of curbside car service. By that time, the once novel idea of the "new motor lunch" had become part and parcel of growing up in America and traveling by car. With an endless parade of imitators, the likes of Pig n' Whistle, Marriott's, Mel's, and many others, carrying on the drive-in dream from coast-to-coast, the drive-in restaurant was poised to remain the foundation of roadside commerce for years to come.

Made famous in the George Lucas film *American Graffiti*, the Mel's Drive-In that was located on San Francisco's South Van Ness was truly the quintessential curb service operation. Today, Steven Weiss continues to operate Mel's units throughout California and to provide the nostalgic atmosphere of the 1950s to modern-day customers. *CoolStock/Steven Weiss photo*

Chapter Two

CARHOPS AND CUSTOMER SERVICE

*B*y the time America's drive-in restaurants reached their zenith in the 1950s, the parking lot server had evolved to become an integral part of the ambiance and pop culture of roadside dining. Eating out in your car meant personal interaction with a carhop—a living, breathing entity with feelings and emotions that catered to every whim when it came to food and drink service along the road.

As we learned in the previous chapter, the story of the first carhops began at the turn of the century when the young lads who were employed at pharmacy soda fountains doubled as deliverymen to carriage-mounted customers at curbside.

As the decades progressed, a small number of businesses experimented with this new format, albeit in a limited fashion. It wasn't until 1921 that the fantasy of being served in one's vehicle by a

The ordering board is used by Sonic drive-ins as a way to show exactly what food and beverage items are available on the menu. The customer depresses a button and addresses a worker inside the building who takes his order. Compared to the other fast food menu boards currently in use, it's a setup that allows the patron some semblance of control.
Michael Karl Witzel

Kim's drive-in is a landmark for car service in Waco, Texas. The town boasts a rich history of drive-in eateries that at one time featured car service by way of carhops. Today, the elaborate Las Vegas-style sign that attracted customers back in the 1950s still shines. *Michael Karl Witzel*

The McDonnell's drive-ins operated in the Los Angeles area circa 1930. The owner, Rusty McDonnell, employed the services of a local artist to sketch whimsical representations of the typical male and female carhop on his menus. Back then paper menus were a large part of dining in a motorcar and took the place of today's impersonal, illuminated menu boards. *Author collection*

waiter gained any great notoriety. By then, the motorcar had entrenched itself in virtually every level of society, and a bond between man and machine had formed. Sure, cars were practical means for getting to and from work, but they also provided one limitless hours of pleasure. Why not consume one's lunch or dinner right behind the steering wheel?

Texas' Pig Stand was the prototype drive-in. With its construction in 1921, a brand new protocol for customer interaction was introduced. As customers in their automobiles pulled up to the curb, young men assigned to serve them eagerly jumped up onto the running boards of the cars before the vehicles even came to a stop! Orders were taken and relayed by foot to the cook shack where the food was prepared. When ready, the barbecued fare—"Pig sandwiches"—were hustled to the customer where they were consumed in the front seat of the automobile. For the busy carhops, speed and agility were of the utmost importance since the wages of drive-in servers in those days consisted entirely of customer tips.

It was this rather aggressive style of automobile service that influenced the creation of the term "carhop" and the widespread acceptance of in-car dining. As more and more drive-in eateries appeared to copy the Pig Stand's great success, Americans were finding out that their cars were ideal facilitators for all sorts of fun and frolic. By the end of the 1920s, drive-ins were well on their

Lorraine Magowan worked as a carhop at the Los Angeles Simon's Drive-In during the late 1930s. At the time most of the curb gals working in the area borrowed their fashion cues from the military and donned the basic hat, slacks, and simple shirt arrangement seen here. *Courtesy Lorraine Magowan*

During the second decade of this century, the carhop, or runner as he was then called, was almost always male. Pharmacies (like this one in Dallas, Texas) employed the services of the soda jerk and later hired dedicated delivery boys to bring liquid refreshments out to the cars. After the majority of men went off to fight in various wars, more women entered the workforce and eventually serving automobiles at the drive-in became the domain of the female. *Dallas Public Library*

way to becoming part of this nation's popular culture. Among the mobile cognoscenti, it was acknowledged that eating in your car with the top down was the preferable way to dine. The high-speed delivery of the always flamboyant carhop readily satisfied the growing demand.

Meanwhile Roy Allen, who was operating a small root beer stand near Lodi, California, began experimenting with the next phase of in-car service—what he called "tray girls." Upon discovering that female servers caused an increase in business, Allen added even more to his staff and watched as his operations grew. By the mid-1930s his A & W Root Beer brand was a household name and throngs of customers were driving out onto the roadways in search of a frosty mug. Of course, some male car owners had ulterior motives: They were venturing out to see the new legion of female carhops strut their stuff.

Since many of the drive-ins across the country were switching to female carhops, that was relatively easy to do. World War II exacerbated the situation as much of the male workforce was shipped overseas leaving women to take over the existing carhop jobs. Before too long, wages at the local drive-in were looking almost as good as those pulled down by "Rosie the Riveter" at the bomber plants in southern California. To earn some extra cash, free hours were soon spent at

Carl's drive-ins of southern California employed carhops who wore elaborate outfits a bit different from the competition. Instead of the usual slack, shirt, and jaunty cap combination that was so common at the time, hops at Carl's were required to wear ruffled skirts. *Security Pacific Historical Photograph Collection*

During the 1950s, Ramona Longpre (center) was the carhop's carhop at Mel's classic drive-in eatery in Berkeley, California. Pictured here in various working situations with her coworkers, the top right image highlights a reunion the curb gals had back in 1988 (from left: Polly, Ramona Longpre, Mary Carrico, and Ollie). All four worked as carhops in the Berkeley area during the heyday of drive-ins. *CoolStock/Ramona Longpre photos*

the local drive-in burger joint jotting down food orders and slinging trays.

Naturally, restaurant proprietors were pleasantly surprised by just how much additional business could be pulled in with female help—especially when that help was outfitted in a revealing costume. Sure, a natty curb boy outfitted with white shirt and black bow tie projected a nice, professional image, but he didn't have nearly the impact of a waitress who sauntered around a parking lot wearing what some publications of the day referred to as "silk pajamas"! That kind of image could really pull 'em in.

One of the most visible developments regarding American carhop fashion occurred in 1938 when J. D. and Louise Sivils opened an elaborate "drive-in" operation in the city of Houston,

Texas. Louise knew exactly what she wanted and her first order of business was to create eye-popping uniforms. Taking inspiration from a series of Chesterfield cigarette ads, she dressed her girls in revamped majorette outfits. An able seamstress, she made the outfits herself and adopted shimmery satin as the material of choice when it came to clothing her "curb girls."

The Sivils garb set the new standard for curb service. Comprised of a tightly fitted majorette-style jacket teamed up with a matching pair of shorts, the set was distinguished by an elaborate plumed hat. Keeping the locality in mind, fancy cowboy boots were used for footwear (new girls

Marbett's was a drive-in restaurant outfit that was a spin-off of the famous White Tower hamburger chain. Their gleaming, porcelain clad, Streamline Moderne buildings were premanufactured by the Valentine Diner Company of Wichita, Kansas. Here, carhops led by their male leader (center) assemble prior to the day's service. *CoolStock/Photo courtesy Tombrock Corporation*

were required to buy their own). Although they made the gals look great, the decorative outfits definitely had drawbacks. During the hot summer months the combination of high-top boots and nonbreathable satin turned many a little girl's dream of car service into a nightmare.

Despite the often uncomfortable working apparel, the allure of becoming a carhop became ever greater. Aided by imaginative operators who turned the simple act of hanging a tray load of hamburgers, Cokes, French fries, and milk shakes on a parked car into a new form of American theater, the drive-in mystique spread like wildfire throughout the country. Suddenly, everyone wanted to get a job at the local drive-in eatery and the position of carhop attained as much status as the job of airline stewardess or nurse. By the time our best and brightest were off to fight a new war

America's choice

Menu
HOWARD JOHNSON'S
delicious food

You and your family will always find a friendly welcome at Howard Johnson's . . . a pleasant atmosphere . . . good food at sensible prices served by a waitress trained to bring you the best in courteous, efficient, friendly service . . . no matter where you travel!

HOWARD JOHNSON'S
RESTAURANTS   MOTOR LODGES
Ice Cream • Candies • Take-Home Frozen Foods
"Landmark for Hungry Americans"
Main offices at 89 Beale Street, Wollaston, Mass., and 40 Rockefeller Plaza, New York 20, N. Y.

Howard Johnson's used to be one of the most popular dining stops to drive into when taking a trip. Although she didn't provide car service, the iconic image of the American waitress was a major selling point for the restaurant chain, as was the 28 flavors of ice cream available within.
Author collection

in Korea, America's carhops were truly the "belles of the boulevard."

After carhop Josephine Powell appeared on the cover of *Life* magazine, the longing for curb jobs turned to a wild frenzy. With all the future beauty queens and debutantes high-stepping around on American parking lots, the drive-in restaurant definitely became the place for those in cars to sit back and watch the show. Suffice it to say that there was many a male hot-rodder who sat in his roadster slowly sipping at a milk shake while dreaming of a date with one of these service celebrities of the strip.

By the end of the 1950s, the stereotypical carhop of the type depicted in the movie *American Graffiti* made her debut at the drive-in. Now she was clad in tight-fitting spandex slacks with a white blouse and jaunty pillbox hat. She had an attitude to match and took full advantage of her newly acquired status. After roller skates were strapped to her feet to make operations move a bit faster, her image transcended from the able car-servant that she was to a full-blown American icon. The car-crazy public that visited drive-ins and wolfed down food in their shiny new automobiles knew what they liked, and this was it.

But in the long run, even the extra speed afforded by roller skates couldn't save carhop service. As the 1960s turned to the 1970s, the pace of life clicked up yet another notch and the public demanded even faster food. Multiple trips made by carhops to take the order, fill it, and return for the tray were viewed as redundant. At the same time, real-estate and other operating costs were rising. To save money, the nation's drive-ins clamored for methods to free them from human tray carriers.

Eventually, speaker box systems using vacuum tubes and miles of wiring replaced carhops, until finally she was the dinosaur of the drive-in trade. A pole-mounted intercom setup superseded all of the ordering duties formerly done in person. A person sitting behind the "drive-thru" window assumed the responsibility of handing out the entrees. With that, the personal touch was gone. The public had come to accept the utility of impersonal gadgetry and had forgotten what it was like to be served by a real person. The era of carhops and customer service was over.

The carhop was a frequent visitor in the print advertisements that were used by the drive-ins down through the ages. Here, the newly improved version of the 1960s A & W carhop has been remade as a streamlined reincarnation of her predecessor, now donning a modern cap that would look at home on any jetliner stewardess or military employee. *Author collection/courtesy A & W Restaurants, Inc.*

Thirst-aid station

A&W ROOT BEER...brewed with pure natural ingredients and true draft flavor ...so good with food!

LOOK FOR THE BRIGHT ORANGE A&W!

Valuable franchises available in the U.S.A. and abroad. Write today A&W ROOT BEER CO.
922 BROADWAY • SANTA MONICA, CALIF.

Fun and refreshments are always ready for you at the 2400 A&W "thirst aid stations" coast-to-coast and overseas. A stop for A&W's delicious food and drinks makes a hit with everyone — even baby (under 5 years) gets a FREE Baby Mug of wholesome natural-ingredient A&W Root Beer with that true *draft* flavor you can't get in bottles or cans. Taste for yourself! It's FREE "Treat-A-Friend" Month at A&W. Bring coupon below for TWO FREE Root Beers at any A&W.

BE A HERO... TAKE HOME A TREAT!

Watch their eyes light up when you bring in that big bright gallon of A&W. (Be sure and take home enough — and don't forget delicious A&W food!)

Copyright, 1965—A&W Root Beer Co.

ALL THE WORLD LOVES A&W!

2400 A&W's Coast-to-Coast and Overseas

215

Chapter Three

THOSE HAVENS FOR HAMBURGERS

Although many of the more elaborate drive-in restaurants in this country boasted a gigantic menu and a seemingly endless variety of foods, it was that American favorite known as the hamburger that rose to fame and fortune along the highways and byways. By the end of the 1960s, the stacked sandwich that could be held in one hand (and eaten while driving) dominated the "fast food" industry. With the approval of the automotive-powered customer, mom and apple pie were muscled out of the kitchen and the hamburger was christened the new icon of American convenience food.

The transformation didn't happen overnight. In the early part of the century, the hamburger was regarded with much suspicion by the general public. No one could really trust what restaurateurs with an eye toward profits were adding to their mixtures of ground meat. The "hamburger sandwich," as it was called in those days, occupied a lowly position on the menus at most greasy spoons across the country.

McDonald's has always been a haven for hamburgers. Back during the 1950s and 1960s, great-looking buildings of the type shown here were the standard issue for franchisees eager to get into the business. Today, the neon-clad dream is over; the environmental look is the new architectural style. *Howard Ande*

217

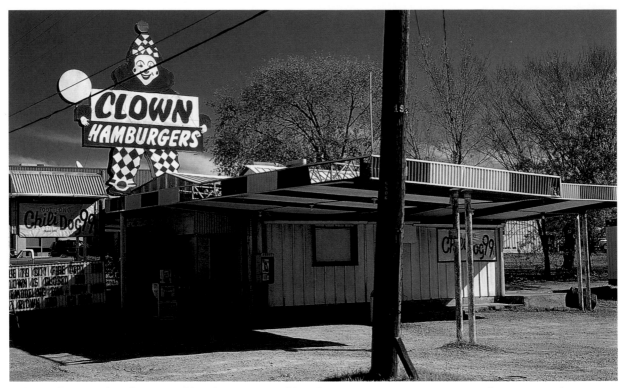

Individually owned and operated hamburger joints like Clown-Burger were at one time the majority along America's roadways. These days, most of the mom-and-pop operations that occupy space along once busy access corridors are closing down, making way for the corporate giants of fast food. This site was recently razed and the clown retired from service. *Michael Karl Witzel*

In 1916, the situation improved slightly after traveling fry cook Walter Anderson opened a tiny, three-stool lunch counter in Wichita, Kansas. The burger operation prided itself on quality ingredients and clean surroundings. After expanding to additional locations, the fledgling chain was named White Castle. It was an appropriate name: gleaming counters and floors gained customer confidence. Food preparation was in full view and everyone could see what was going into their lunches and how they were made. Unlike a few other places of ill-repute, burger patties that dropped to the floor were never picked up, dusted off, and slapped between a bun for the next unsuspecting customer to purchase.

As White Castles spread across the United States and similar operations opened for business, the regional bill of fare that typified the roadside food of the 1920s began a slow change. Gradually, the hamburger gained enthusiastic converts and worked its way into the hierarchy of foods. While the blue-plate special (with all the trimmings) remained the top entree at sit-down restaurants, operations that added on drive-in service began to augment their menus with new edibles. More motorists were asking for burgers, and it seemed a logical choice when one considered that it had to be eaten in cramped quarters. The combination of ground meat and a bun was an almost perfect design.

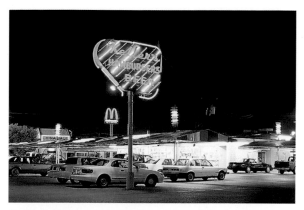

Keller's Hamburgers is a surviving drive-in that does a booming business in the city of Dallas, Texas. A prodigious amount of neon lighting has made this burger stop a local landmark and this colorful sign pulls in traffic. *Michael Karl Witzel*

Every so often, a trip along the back roads of America reveals a drive-in or hamburger stand that isn't recognized by the consumer force-fed with continual television commercials and motion-picture cross-promotions. These are the places that one may get some of the best road food around. *Michael Karl Witzel*

In effect, the hamburger was a full-course meal without all the pomp and circumstance of the sit-down dinner. Unlike the loose meat sandwich, the circular hamburger stuck together (the addition of melted cheese helped). Because of its symmetrical properties, it could be attacked from any direction and rotated to suit one's fancy. Cheap chuck meat provided a protein source that was just as good as pot roast or steak, while simple toppings replaced the usual appetizers and dinner salad. Rather than being served in a table basket, buns could be integrated into the total package as well. Finally, hurried diners had a portable meal that contained fortifying items from all the major food groups.

Both drive-in proprietors and their patrons recognized the convenience, and by the 1940s the hamburger had gained a marked level of respectability along the roadways. While many a curb stand still served the various local specialties, the burger and its numerous iterations became a staple food. Many incarnations were tried, including double-meat stackups, cheeseburgers, chiliburgers, and more. Even so, a basic ingredient roster and preparation method emerged, defined by

ground meat, bun, pickles, lettuce, tomato, and onions. Add-on condiments such as ketchup, mustard, and mayonnaise were slathered on in varying proportions, according to customer demand.

With the hot sandwich made of ground beef becoming the core of their business, the majority of drive-in restaurants in America became havens for hamburgers. Suddenly, frazzled commuters were ordering an inordinate number of these hot, circular sandwiches, forsaking the elaborate trout dinners, specially prepared soups, and other time-consuming entrees that they once gobbled down with glee. Life was getting faster and complicated all the way around, and as a result, affordable, portable, palatable food that could keep up with the times was poised for greatness.

A few drive-in operators with vision saw that the future of fast food was in the burger and decided that they would make it the basis for their entire business. Robert Wian was one of the first burgermeisters to gain fame, opening a small five-stool lunch counter in Glendale, California. In the winter of 1937, he was working the serving counter at Bob's Pantry when late-night customer Stewie Strange requested "something different." Wian

During the 1950s, the Harry Hines strip in Dallas, Texas, was the top place to cruise if you wanted to visit a drive-in. Although most of the classics are gone, the Prince of Hamburgers is one burger joint that remains. *Michael Karl Witzel*

cooked to please and the impromptu burger that sizzled off of the griddle became the signature two-story cheeseburger that earned him his reputation and promised to make his drive-ins a success.

At the time, six-year-old local boy Richard Woodruff was a regular customer at Bob's place. Woodruff was always looking for a free food hand-out, and occasionally, Wian let him sweep the floors or do some other odd job in exchange for a snack. Charmed by his droopy overalls, pudgy physique, and limitless appetite for grilled beef patties, Wian decided to call his new, multilevel sandwich the "Big Boy." Later, a local cartoonist sketched a rendition of the hungry street urchin on a napkin, and before the decade was done, the lad with tousled hair, red-and-white checked over-alls, and pot belly was a trademark adorning advertising signs, burger wrappers, and even the front facade of Wian's burger joint.

Aided by the memorable images of the Big Boy, news of the "double-deck" cheeseburger spread far and wide, and by the 1950s, Wian was franchising the tasty Big Boy sandwich and its

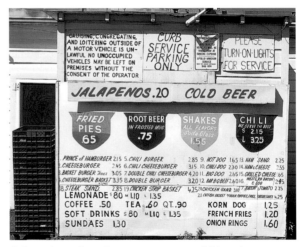

A few short decades ago, a successful hamburger seller need two things to remain profitable: a great roadside sign and good food. Today it's becoming extremely difficult for the individual operator to survive with only these two attributes. National advertising and name recognition have become an unfortunate requirement of the business. *Michael Karl Witzel*

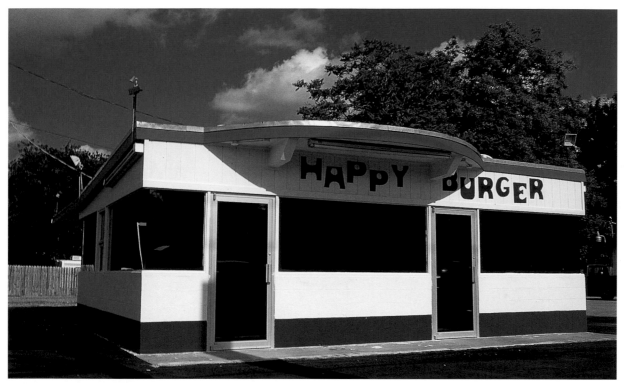

In Sapulpa, Oklahoma, the Happy Burger that's doing business along old Highway 66 attempts to attract its patrons with a decidedly patriotic color scheme. Flamboyant paint is nothing new; burger joints have tried every trick in the book to get cars to stop and take a taste of their ground chuck sandwiches. *Jim Ross*

amusing trademark to restaurateurs in six states. Twenty years later, the portly kid was greeting customers nationwide. By that time, he had grown to become a larger-than-life statue sculpted of painted fiberglass, holding a deluxe cheeseburger platter high in the sky for all those passing to see. With a flavor unmatched, the Big Boy drive-ins went big time and carhops scurried about on the parking lots to meet the demand.

But Robert Wian wasn't the only one jumping on the hamburger bandwagon. Around the same time the Big Boy creation was gaining fans, Richard and Maurice McDonald were busy creating their own hamburger legacy. It all started when the pair were employed in Hollywood transporting movie sets. After taking notice of a local hot dog vendor who was doing a bang-up business, they quit their jobs to try their hand at the drive-in game. In 1937, they opened a small orange juice stand on Highway 66 and three years later, moved the octagonal unit to a better sales location in San Bernardino. For the next 11 years, they perfected their carhop operation until they could improve it no more.

In 1948 they decided that major changes were needed, and they temporarily closed the eatery. A few months later, they reopened with a more efficient operation. To their regular customers' great concern and shock, carhop service was eliminated, along with the once varied food items, the real silverware, the plates, and the choices! Along with fries, soda pop, and milk shakes, nothing but hamburgers would be served. Customers were required to make (and pick up) orders at walk-up windows. The McDonalds called this streamlined arrangement the "Speedy Service System."

Many of the classic, circular hamburger havens that copied the basic design of the ground beef sandwich were a great place to go inside and sit down—especially if the cold winter temperatures made the cheese on your cheeseburger turn as stiff as cardboard. *University of Louisville Ekstrom Library*

In 1940, the McDonald brothers sliced the "Airdrome" refreshment stand in two pieces and transported it to a new site located at 14th and E streets in San Bernardino, California. It was remodeled, and 20 carhops with satin uniforms were hired. On weekend nights, 125 cars touched fenders in the parking lot of this drive-in classic. *Richard McDonald collection*

After a brief drop in business, the concept really took off. In spite of the limited variations offered, hurried customers found the service to be impeccable and the food to be pretty good. Consumption of the hamburger sandwich that they had unanimously elected as the nation's favorite road food was now more convenient than ever! In exchange for the slightly more rigid business format, hurried diners could take advantage of economical pricing, lightning-quick service, and total convenience. Best of all, there was absolutely no tipping of carhops required!

Sometime later, salesman Ray Kroc discov-ered the magic of the setup, and in partnership with the McDonalds, took the idea of the fast food hamburger nationwide. By the time the 1960s were over, the mighty hamburger had spread across the land with little restraint, annihilating all of the homemade recipes and regional folk foods that were once eaten and adored by the cross-country traveler. Duplicated by an endless string of imitators, the "franchised" fast food hamburger became the body snatcher of the roadside restaurant. In time, America would be oblivious to the qualities of drive-in dining that once made the act of consuming them so much fun in the first place.

Bob's Big Boy was quite fond of hamburgers and made it known that the grilled patty sandwich was a favorite of his. Clutching the proverbial double-deck burger in his hand, he graced the covers of menus for years. *Author collection*

Texas artist Randy Welborn has adopted the drive-in restaurant as a favorite motif for his evocative paintings of the American roadside. The circular Pig Stand drive-in shown in this scene is still a working operation that serves patrons in the city of Beaumont, Texas. *Randy Welborn*

225

Chapter Four

EVOLVING AMERICAN CURB FOOD

Although the hamburger sandwich has remained the paramount road food for more than four decades, many a motorist in search of quick sustenance along America's highways and byways has discovered that there's more to life than just a chunk of ground beef slapped between two halves of a bun. As the hamburger made its meteoric rise to the top of the junk food heap, a myriad of other portable foods that were easy to prepare, inexpensive to buy, and delightful to the taste buds found their own success along the roadways. Not surprisingly, they are still thriving today.

The big question: How did these other popular food entrees get a foothold in the business of roadside food? The answer is simple. Many got their start long before the automobile was accepted as a practical mode of transportation and as a direct result, were perfected by the time the internal-combustion engine permanently replaced horse power.

Susie's Drive-Thru is one of the finer fast food spots along Chicago's Montrose Avenue. Rather than serve up the same old fare, Philadelphia beefsteak sandwiches are a specialty here, offering motorists a chance to taste something other than the burger-and-fry combination. *Howard Ande*

Joliet, Illinois, is the place to find delicious Polish hot dogs when you're speeding in an automobile down Route 30. Naturally, it's also a good place to get a hamburger, as indicated by this neon-sign beauty captured at dusk. *Howard Ande*

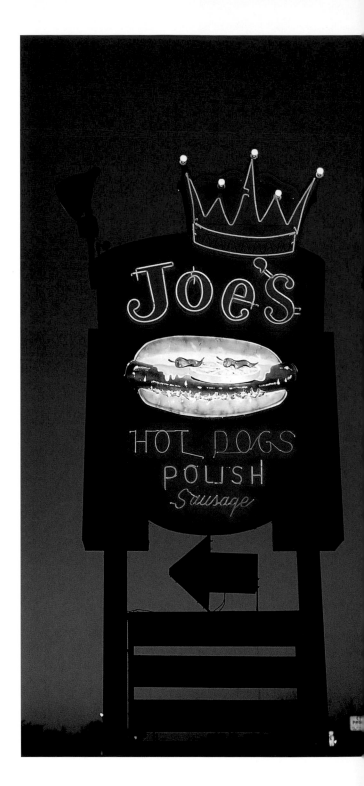

When the motorcar became a common transit appliance, those food items that meshed with three very important criteria were poised for gastrointestinal greatness.

Among these important determining factors was the innate ability of a food item to be carried aboard an automobile without any additional fuss or bother. Warming pots, large serving tureens, or other such gadgets that were found in the finest kitchens of the day were not at all acceptable. Along with grandma's recipe book and well-stocked larder, there was no place for a cast-iron stove or pile of firewood in a motorcar—unless one was piloting a steam-powered vehicle.

In addition to portability, entrees that aspired to become the favored food of automobilists had to possess the unique attributes that allowed them to be consumed with neither knife nor fork. With that in mind, a successful car food placed minimal demand on the driver's manual dexterity. In light of unwieldy steering wheels (no hydraulic assist), starting cranks, dashboard levers, gearshifts, and other appendages that had to be controlled while in transit, it was a definite necessity that food taken on the road be easy to hold—and eat—with just one hand. If it could be consumed with a few large bites, all the better.

Since the upscale city restaurants, wayside inns, and well-appointed "tearooms" of the second and third decades were often rather expensive affairs, cost became a consideration in the formulation of successful roadway fare as well. The enthusiastic motorist of the day was required to spend a considerable amount of cash on the repair and upkeep of the motor vehicle. Consequently, all of the many food items that were to be considered as candidates for mass consumption along the nation's traffic corridors had to be economical and affordable.

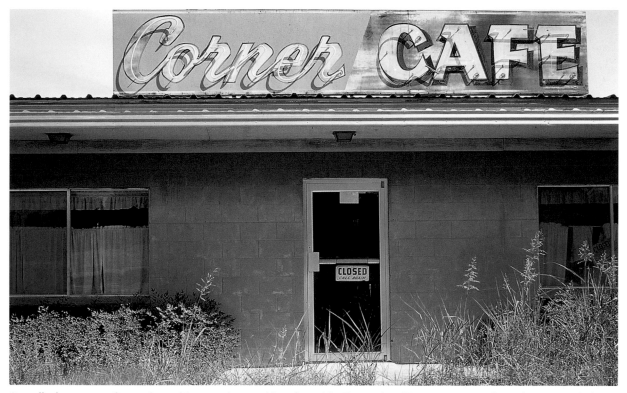

So-called corner cafes such as this pastel apparition found in Grapevine, Texas, are a modern-day rarity. Only small towns and out of the way places that time has forgotten allow operations such as these to thrive—and serve food. *Michael Karl Witzel*

Even after meeting these varied guidelines, there remained one more need to be satisfied: Meals that were to be consumed by the cross-country adventurer had to be highly accessible. Motoring was still somewhat of a dirty hobby from 1910 until the early 1920s, and more often than not, it resulted in the participants getting soiled with dust, spattered with grease, or stained with gasoline. While they were wearing the dusters, goggles, and heavy gauntlets required by open roadster driving, enthusiasts were often reluctant to step into a "civilized" inn to request food and beverage. For the ardent automobilist, picnic baskets were all the rage.

Fortunately, there were a few operators of the time who perceived the growing demand for fast food that was served away from the home.

Using whatever culinary and marketing skills they had at hand, they rose to the challenge of feeding the growing motoring masses. At first, so-called greasy spoons and dining shacks known as "beaneries" sprang up—usually near the towns that hosted large factory facilities and a substantial amount of industrial workers who needed to take their lunch away from home.

Here, an assortment of basic food items (all using cheap ingredients requiring minimal culinary skill to prepare) like chili, beans, soups, and stews were served up. For the assembly-line worker who toiled across the street and needed a fast lunch, the arrangement was acceptable. But these low-buck joints were not geared to the free-wheeling motorist. All of these facilities demanded that customers arriving by foot or car sit down at a table or counter.

The roadside diners, cafes, restaurants, and drive-ins of America were once great places to hear your favorite singing group. When inside seating was available, booths were almost always outfitted with jukebox controllers that provided three plays for a quarter. Often, the selection of songs available was as eclectic as the many choices on the food menu. *Michael Karl Witzel*

Serving beer used to be a really big deal at drive-in restaurants like Keller's in Dallas. In order to get around local ordinances that made certain areas "dry," operators often moved outside the city limits so that the frothy brew could still flow freely to the customers who wanted it. *Michael Karl Witzel*

Leslie's Chicken Shack was a Waco, Texas, restaurant that employed curb service for a number of years. Serving "California-style" fried chicken, the eatery opened operations in nearby cities and continued to maintain this unit until recent years. Now, the famous chicken sign and building are up for sale. Another unique roadside food has gone extinct.
Michael Karl Witzel

While Harlan Sanders, the "Colonel," is best known for his secret Kentucky Fried Chicken recipe, there remains a gaggle of drive-ins throughout the states that serve up fowl with equal flavor. This Chicken 'n Dip serves both ice cream and bird and is located along Route 72 in Hampshire, Illinois.
Howard Ande

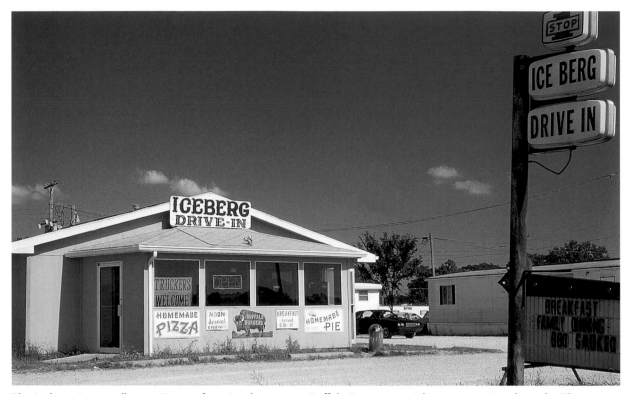

The Iceberg is a small-town Kansas favorite that uses a Buffalo Burger specialty to attract its clientele. The citizens of Fredonia (and those just passing through) visit it often for the unusual bill of fare served there. *Michael Karl Witzel*

As more and more of these lunch spots opened for business, problems with sanitation, hygiene, and food storage began to cast a dark shadow on the low-cost dining routine. Seventy-five years ago, the healthful tenets of food service that are followed today were seldom adhered to at many of these one-man stands. With only crude methods established for food preservation and a total lack of refrigeration, many of these dining establishments gained a somewhat dubious reputation regarding the quality (and sometimes taste) of their food.

Because many of these unsophisticated restaurants were mom-and-pop enterprises with little capital at their disposal, the personnel that prepared the food often lacked training in the art of cookery. Irrespective of cold sandwiches (not as popular then as they are today), people demanded hot things to fill up their bellies. As a result, the select recipes that could be created with great haste were often centered around some sort of integrated food item that was made from a mixture of ingredients. Ground beef or pork—in the form of circular patties, meatballs, or cased sausage—was seen as the perfect fodder for the untrained chef.

Unfortunately, these ingredient caused a few problems with quality. Many turn-of-the-century proprietors took advantage of the opportunity and adulterated their products with additional fat, filler, and inferior additives. Unlike a bowl of beef stew or beans that could be carefully examined as each of the individual spoonfuls was lifted toward the mouth, bites that were taken directly from encapsulated food items left scant opportunity for

At the Hot Shoppes, barbecue made of ham and pork shoulders was the main bill of fare. With hot sauce and relish, it sold for 30 cents during the 1950s. The famous milkshake was next; at 25 cents it got the motorists' attention more often than root beer. As thick as a frappe, it was modeled after the delicious shakes made at the Brigham Drugstore in Salt Lake City where young J. Willard Marriott attended college. Although gas rationing blacked out curbing for several years during the war, these staple entrees never lost favor with the public. By the 1950s, 2,000,000 barbecues and 2,300,000 milkshakes were sold per year. The question was, who came up with the trademark orange roof first, Mr. Marriott or Mr. Johnson? *Bob Sigmon collection*

a detailed examination. It was ironic indeed that the very attributes that made hamburgers and hot dogs a perfect choice for car food also relegated them to a questionable status. Until improvements were instituted throughout the industry as a whole, the convenience of dining along the highways and byways were overshadowed by cases of stomach cramps and intestinal distress.

Those changes were quick in coming, as more and more automobiles hit the streets, the unscrupulous minority of food concessionaires were effectively forced to change, or exit the business. By the early 1920s respectable drive-in

restaurants like the Texas Pig Stands began to appear on the American roadside with greater frequency. Gradually, they altered the course of roadside dining and began repairing the damage done by their unsavory predecessors. With an eye toward expanding operations nationwide, these roadside upstarts initiated a trend that diverged from the saucy variety of sit-down foods that the majority of lunch counters were serving and opted for meals that could be eaten with more ease.

By maintaining simple menus and featuring one food item as their specialty, they were better able to get a handle on the variables that caused

When Roy Allen and Frank Wright teamed up to sell root beer in the early 1920s, they decided to combine their initials and form a new company name. A & W was the result, incorporated into a graphic symbol featuring the now-familiar "pointing arrow." Since the day the first frosty mug was sold in 1919, a mug of A & W Root Beer could be purchased for just one nickel. By the time World War II broke out, the "5-cent" circle was as much a symbol of A & W as the orange-and-black logo divided with an arrow. (Notice the direction.) *A & W Restaurants Inc.*

Chicken in the Rough was invented in 1936 by Mr. and Mrs. Beverly Osborne. They ran a small Oklahoma City drive-in and franchised their tasty poultry dish to operators nationwide. Consisting of one-half a golden brown chicken served with shoestring potatoes, hot buttered biscuits, and a jug 'o honey, it was a meal served without silverware. In 1958, a Chicken in the Rough platter could be purchased for $1.40 Tuesday through Sunday. It was reduced to $1.00 on Monday, which was family night. *Jim Ross*

foods to become tainted in the first place and at the same time control quality. Barbecued "pig sandwiches" were a great choice, for example, since the meat used to make them was maintained at the proper temperature in a large smoker. At the same time, bread was delivered daily and soft drinks were served out of sealed bottles. The popular press took notice of the many drive-on success stories, and as the incidents of ptomaine poisoning declined, the notion of the specialized food stand gained increased acceptance with America's motorists.

Curiously enough, the same convenience foods that were once regarded with suspicion rose to the top of the table in roadside fare. By way of the drive-in restaurant, selections that were affordable and could be prepared quickly became the standards for a nation that was inebriated by the limitless freedoms afforded by the automobile. The ability to wolf a hot dog, chomp on a hamburger, or gnaw on a basket of fried chicken was appreciated by the open roadster crowd that had little time to waste with the excessive formality of dining in an indoor eatery.

Chapter Five

DRIVE-IN DIVERSITY

*T*oday, the architecture of roadside food operations has reached a defined level of banality. It all started during the 1970s when operators decided that it was no longer acceptable to look just like a plain old burger joint. Exterior panels of porcelain enamel were removed, neon signs were taken down, and unusual design qualities muted. Suddenly, hamburger huts that catered to car customers were required to "blend in" with the environment.

All at once, the commercial design motifs that had served the public for so many years were deemed outmoded. In the rush to upgrade and constantly create a new and improved image to their expanding customer base, the brain trust at the helm of America's restaurant concerns decided that drastic changes were in order. The postwar configurations that had brought them so

The city of Great Bend, Kansas, is the place to be driving if you are searching for a genuine example of programmatic drive-in architecture. Today, a surviving Twistee Treat ice cream stand illuminates the night and does a brisk business from within a colorful building that's shaped like an ice cream cone and hot fudge sundae rolled into one.
Howard Ande

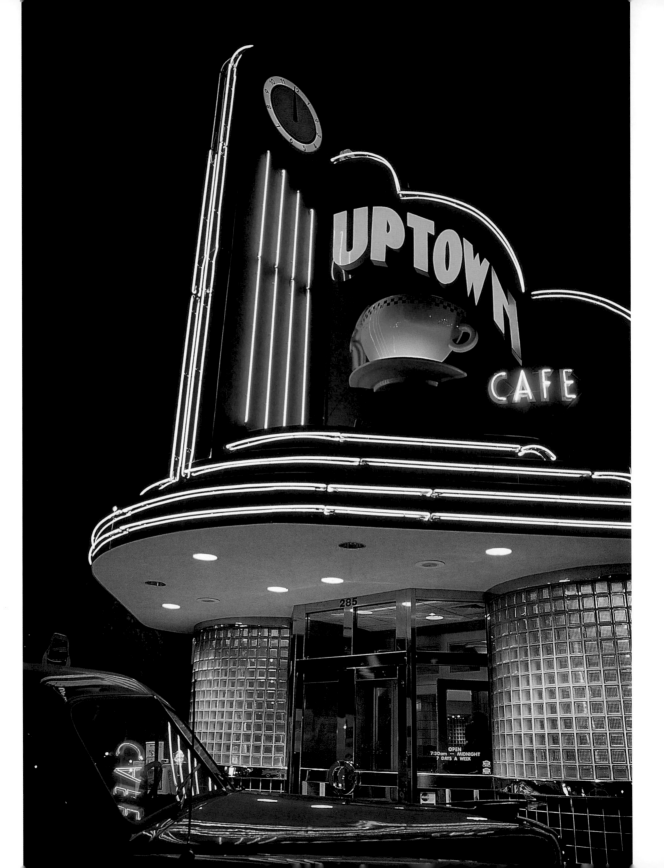

much success were to be re-engineered and redirected to project a softer, more friendly attitude to the general public.

This kinder and gentler architectural slant resulted in the hasty demolition and remodeling of some of our nation's best examples of drive-in design. With little protest mounted by customers, the gleaming boxes of bright porcelain enamel were hastily resurfaced with brick. Flat roofs and dramatic advertising pylons that once captured imaginations were now considered passé and the simple mansard roof emerged as the new favorite. The chrome-plated look that was so indicative of yesteryear was dramatically dropped. Natural woods of every imaginable type became the universal replacement.

Out on the restaurant parking lots, it was no longer enough to provide a clear, flat, accessible pad for the arriving automobiles. Landscaping was taken to the extreme, characterized by a maze of predetermined driving lanes and decorative greenery that was integrated into the total restaurant package. Now, the burger-and-fry bunch were to imagine that they were visiting just another comfortable home in the neighborhood, complete with all the trappings of suburbia. At the same time, a separate playground area for the children became a prerequisite to convenience dining as well. Meticulously maintained lawns (emulating a golfing green), fine trimmed shrubbery, and decorative flowers of the finest variety completed the bucolic fast food illusion of the new age.

Seventy-five years ago, the entrepreneurs who were eager to reap the benefits of the automobile were not so concerned with finding an architectural aesthetic that appealed to the universal mind. In those early days of the drive-in, most wayside dining operations that served the newfan-

Elaborate architectural beauties like the Uptown Cafe in Branson, Missouri, routinely use the building styles that made the drive-in restaurant such a major attraction. Glass block, neon tubing, and polished metal are some of the elements that recall the crazy days of carhops and curb service. *Howard Ande*

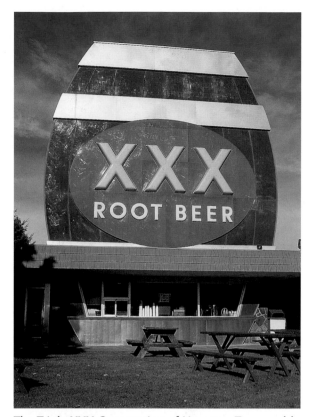

The Triple XXX Corporation of Houston, Texas, sold a lot of root beer during the 1930s and 1940s. Outlets were generally located in the Western half of the states, with a profusion of locations stretching from California and Washington. Key to the operation were buildings incorporating a giant root beer barrel. Many featured larger-than-life renditions—while some (such as this Washington State version) added a false front facade shaped like a barrel. As the slogan said: Triple XXX "Makes Thirst a Joy." *Michael Karl Witzel*

gled horseless machines were tentative constructions at best. The motorcar was still an unproven machine, and the outlay of large cash investments in hope of snaring this new market was risky. Unadorned shacks and shanties built with available lumber and "found" materials ruled the day.

There was one practical reason for this rather naive design philosophy: At the turn of the century,

In Globe, Arizona, a teepee-shaped pizza restaurant ekes out an existence. While more than 75 years ago the idea of a building as sign was all the rage, today it's not so appealing. The motoring public has become jaded to out-of-scale structure, and the elaborate signboard has assumed the responsibility of highway marketing.
Michael Karl Witzel

The Mammoth Orange stand drive-in operation was established by Peggy Doler, now retired and living at Garden Grove, California. During the 1940s, she began the operation in her front yard to take advantage of the business rolling by on Highway 99. With the arrival of the new freeway, she was bypassed. As her lifeline was redesignated Chowchilla Boulevard, business dropped. Doler moved the hut to its present site in 1953, and five years ago Jim and Doris Stiggins purchased it. Today, truck drivers still ask about Doler and reminisce about the days when the spring opening meant free food for all of the truckers. Some customers say they have been stopping there for more than 25 years. Baby-boomers recall wheeling in for a chilled flagon of juice with their parents! Taste buds never forget. *Glen Icanberry*

roadside operators were rather inexperienced when it came to appearances. With the automotive industry still in its infancy, there were no franchising guidelines to show them what to do, no books written on the subject outlining the fine points of roadside salesmanship, and no great business leaders to serve as mentors. As a result, those who wanted to get into the fledgling drive-in restaurant business had to make things up as they went along—discovering the hard way what would and wouldn't work.

The passage of years proved that the automobile was definitely here to stay. When the car replaced the horse for good, businessmen began investing ever larger sums of money into their roadside endeavors. By the end of the 1920s, the economic prosperity and giddiness of the times was reflected along the nation's roadsides. "Programmatic" architecture began to appear with more and more frequency, characterized by roadside structures that broke all the rules of conventional building design. Whimsical themes, crazy concepts, and other personal flights of fantasy were made into three-dimensional structures to sell food.

With eye-appeal that promised to draw in car customers like bees to honey, the drive-in restau-

California architect Wayne McAllister's simple circular structure (popularized by restaurateurs operating during the 1930s) has even influenced styles across the Atlantic. Copenhagen, Denmark, is home to the Cafe Around the World, a drive-in throwback that features both indoor and patio dining. The neon advertises a popular Danish beverage, Tuborg beer. *Michael Karl Witzel*

rant was ideally suited to the flamboyant style of programmatic architecture. Limited only by the imagination of those who constructed them, buildings of every conceivable type appeared along the highways: To drive home the fact that sudsy beverages were their mainstay drink, operations such as A & W Root Beer erected fantastic stands that resembled gigantic root beer barrels! At the same time, they experimented with even more mesmerizing, out-of-proportion constructions such as oversized Indian chiefs and scaled-down lighthouses.

Captivated by the dramatic effect of these attention-getting designs, imitators such as the famed Triple XXX root beer stand (located on Waco's busy traffic circle) added oversized kegs as an adjunct to their structure. Animals and other familiar creatures became favorite drive-in motifs as well. By the end of the 1920s, it wasn't unusual to snack on a hamburger at a diner shaped like a giant toad or even a pig. Typically, the program that defined the shape of a food or drink building was indicative of the food specialty served there.

In spite of its strong visual appeal, the "building as sign" motif eventually faded, and by the 1930s the business of the drive-in restaurant was well established in America. With rising competition and the need to turn over customers with increased speed, more serious styles of restaurant architecture were being considered. Unlike those early pioneers who simply threw up a wooden shack and a few hand-painted signs (and opened for business the very next day), modern restaurateurs began looking in earnest toward the professional architects for the answers they needed.

With its expansive boulevards and weather

Highway 54 used to be the main route entering Kansas from the east. Before the freeways, it was the conduit to Wichita—thick with roadside businesses eager to cater to the motorist. Today, this strip of asphalt known as "The Yellow Brick Road" is a living museum of roadside attractions. *Michael Karl Witzel*

conducive to year-round drive-in dining, southern California led the way with designs that were completely dedicated to car food service. Architects implemented a new-and-improved vision for car commerce, and by World War II they had established the "circular" style drive-in as the reigning standard. Appropriately, the balanced-wheel motif proved to be the perfect configuration to sell drive-in car dining to the rest of the nation—incorporating into one flamboyant package all of the attention-getting elements needed to pull paying customers off the streets.

Before too long, nearly every major street corner in Los Angeles played host to a circular drive-in restaurant. From the vantage point of the busy boulevard, these dramatic sculptures of chrome, glass, and stainless steel were truly a sight to behold. Free-floating roof overhangs appeared to defy the laws of gravity as extravagant center spires shot skyward, heavily bedecked with miles of neon tubing. The unified look that was offered by this circular arrangement transformed what was at one time a mundane roadside concession stand into an attractive space station for cars.

Still, there was more substance to the circular design than just heightened visual aesthetics. Ever since the days of the first curbside dining stand, problems with traffic flow and serving logistics had been major concerns. A round design was perfectly suited for roadside dining; with unprece-

When man's race for space began influencing the way designers perceived architecture and automobiles, subtle reminders of that hopeful futurism began appearing as embellishments. While motorcars grew tailfins and rocket-like protrusions, roadside stands such as this Virginia U. S. 1 Dairy Bar added modernistic structural elements. *Michael Karl Witzel*

dented ease, drivers could access the parking lot, cruise around the building's periphery, and quickly shoot into a parking spot that suited their fancy (the "inner circle" became the place to be). Because every dining space was nearly an equal distance from the kitchen, the carhops were better able to maximize their movements.

With the acceptable range of drive-in architecture widened by a few architects with great vision, restaurant operators located in other regions of the country were liberated to interpret their very own way-out drive-in restaurant dreams. And they proceeded to do exactly that, incorporating dramatically stacked layers into their overall building design. By the conclusion of the 1930s, electrical illumination schemes, glass blocks, porcelain enameled panels, streamlining effects, flashing neon, polished metal alloys, stucco exteriors, protective overhead car canopies, elaborate tilework, concrete parking lots, automated serving gadgets, and much, much more had been tried.

Without a doubt, the drive-in restaurant had come a long way and would remain the architectural gem of the American roadside for decades. Taking prominence over the hotel, motel, and gasoline service station, the buildings that allowed patrons to eat in their cars had become an inseparable part of pop culture.

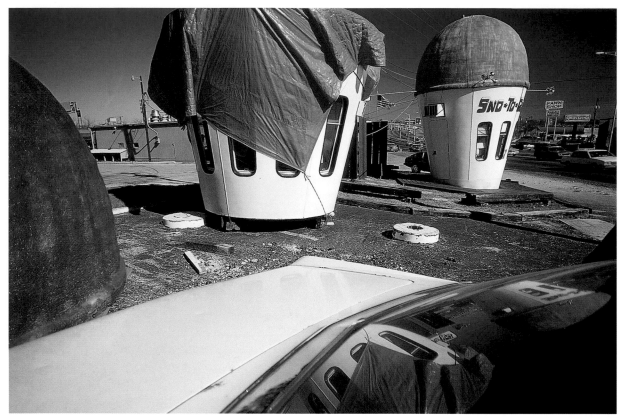

Playing on the visual and verbal language that influences through unconscious association, the imagery of the sno-cone stand captures our attention. "Hey, look at me" is their flashy call to travelers on the open road. In their attempt to break through the insistent cacophony of competing roadside images, they easily succeed. We are lured from the speeding fast track to enjoy the tasty wares of this unique curbside attraction. As synthesis of sign and building, their mimetic form of architectural design reeks of pure kitsch. *Michael Karl Witzel*

The Streamliner Diner Drive-In was one of those cool roadside eateries of yesteryear that made you want to stop just because it looked intriguing. Not only was it a restaurant and a diner, but it also featured carhop car service right from an adjoining drive-in. The train has always been a popular motif for eateries and even today, one may find theme restaurants housed in retired boxcars, old engines, and more. *Author collection*

Seattle's Igloo Drive-In was a well-known attraction during the 1940s. Inside seating for 70 customers made the dual-domed wonder an attractive destination for those who liked to eat in an enclosed dining room. Under the stars, wintertime carhops wore ski-togs from Nordstrom with high white boots and in summertime, short skirts. Owners Ralph Grossman and Ernie Hughes recruited most of the good-looking girls from the local theaters to work there as carhops. *CoolStock/Ralph Grossman photo*

Chapter Six

CRUISING THE MAIN FOR CURB SERVICE

More than any other roadside business in American history, the drive-in restaurant occupied a unique position in the continually evolving culture of the automobile. From the early days of the 1920s until its rapid fall from grace during the 1960s, the curb-service eatery held the distinction of being *the* universal meeting place for this nation's youth.

While the prewar decades saw their share of revelers whooping it up at the nation's drive-in diners, it was the generation that came of age during the 1950s that latched onto the idea of in-car dining with a fervor like no other. And why not? The promises of postwar prosperity were directly reflected in the drive-ins of America. Colorful bands of neon advertised that "happy days are here again," and natty carhops zipping about on roller skates conveyed a reassuring sense of order.

Under the canopy is the place you want to be if you want to be part of the main action that's going on at Keller's Dallas, Texas, drive-in restaurant. Just like during the 1950s, cars jockey for position in the service lanes as the day turns to dusk. By nightfall, a variety of hot rods and street machines may sometimes be seen there. *Michael Karl Witzel*

251

Along Route 66 in Seligman, Arizona, Juan Delgadillo entertains (and feeds) customers at the Sno-Cap Drive-In. Over the last few years, it's become a favorite drive-in destination for people who are cruising along the "Mother Road" and wish to stop and grab a taste of yesterday. *Howard Ande*

Always first to catch (or create) a new trend, American youth quickly adopted the drive-in as their personal stomping grounds and welcomed it into their clique with open arms. When they weren't sleeping, attending school, studying, or playing sports, the parking lot at the local drive-in restaurant was their favorite haunt. There, young adults finding their own way in an adult's world could meet with old friends, find new ones, seek romance, and pursue all of the many social activities that define teenhood.

At the same time, they could escape the confines of the suburban dining room and get a break from the same old meatloaf and mashed potato dinners. By the mid-1950s, American drive-in restaurants were bypassing many of the elaborate entrees of their restaurant brethren in favor of the "junk foods" that kids adored. The fact that burgers and fries were greasy and not particularly healthful for a growing body was inconsequential. Soda pop overloaded with sugar, you say? It simply wasn't an issue in those days. Drive-in food was fun to eat and virtually impossible to get at home.

But there were even more important aspects of the drive-in restaurant that ensured its success as a central gathering place. Around the circular hub of the service wheel, teenagers could congregate with others who believed in the same things that they believed in and who spoke the same language. Almost every high school had a favorite

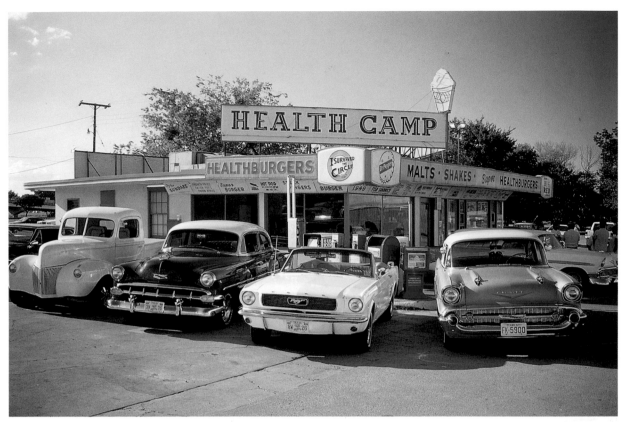

The Healthcamp Drive-In is a modern-day eatery that's a favorite with cruisers in Waco, Texas. An outfit that calls itself "The Heart of Texas Street Machines" has adopted the eatery on the circle as their favorite destination. *Michael Karl Witzel*

drive-in that they adopted as their own. On any given moment of any given day, somebody from school could be found parked there. After school, the local drive-in appeared to be a magnet for cars. From far and wide, participants from all social and cultural backgrounds were drawn to the brightly lit canopies for a few enjoyable hours of food, good times, and fun.

And great fun it was, especially if the pastime known as "cruising" was involved. Enjoyed even before the car existed, albeit in a somewhat more refined form, cruising evolved to become a purely American activity that involved a central strip of in-town roadway and an automobile (a full tank of gas

definitely helped the proceedings). To participate, teens piled into a car, preferably a cool-looking one, and drove around to the many hot spots situated nearby. Usually a major part of this localized road trip involved a slow crawl down the main street corridor. The object was to see and be seen.

As the night's cruising progressed, highly favored routes of travel, or "loops" as they were called, were devised by the participants. Along the way, the many drive-in restaurants that opened for business during the 1950s provided the perfect place to stop and regroup. Because they were the most visible venues at which to be seen and the most likely spots to elicit reactions from others,

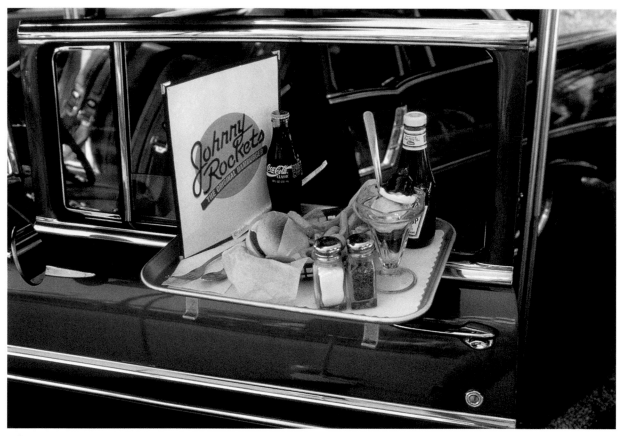

When vehicles are parked at a cruise night or other car show, their owners often mount car service trays—complete with wax foods and other drink replicas—to bring about the atmosphere of the American drive-in restaurant. Cruising and curb service are forever linked in the mind of the cruiser. *Kent Bash*

drive-ins became an important part of "shooting the loop." While cruising the main street strip was fun, nothing compared to the many activities that were going on down at the neighborhood Mel's, Duke's, or Cappy's.

Because of the conspicuous theater that they provided, the goal of cruising was to visit as many drive-in restaurants as possible in a single night. From dusk until the wee hours of the morning (when all the joints closed), cruisers flitted from one drive-in to the next and rode the same track into the dawn until the route was burned into memory like a phonograph needle stuck in the groove of a record.

Cruising was more than just the opportunity to make appearances, however. A big part of the pastime was the serious quest to meet members of the opposite sex. In a never-ending quest for love (or even just a glance) in the fast lane, guys in souped-up hot rods revved their engines at the lights and preened with all the bravado that they could muster, just to attract some girl's attention. At the same time, gals cruised the streets in their own cars (or mom and dad's) to be pursued. The final moves in this age-old game of pursuit and courtship were played out beneath the flickering marquee of the American drive-in restaurant.

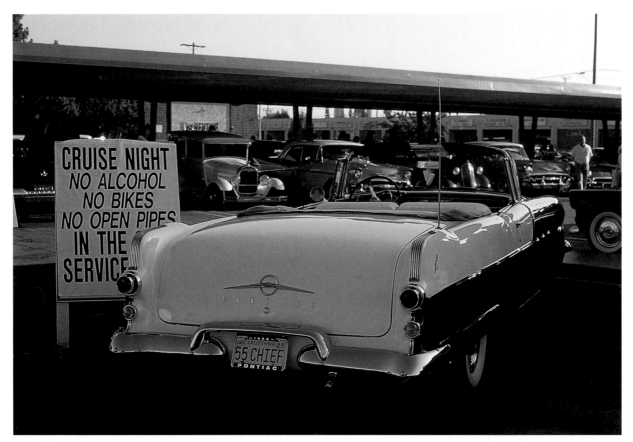

In California, the "cruise night" has become a regular part of the weekend. Every Saturday night, the owners of classic hot rods and custom cars take their prized possessions out of the garage and drive it to their nearest drive-in. Until late night, they eat, talk, and reminisce about the "good old days." *Kent Bash*

While boy-meets-girl dramas played out around them, other drive-in revelers pursued more dangerous games under the auspices of outdoor automotive dining. Most visible among these secondary activities was the obsessive desire of young men to compete with one another. When automobiles were involved, that competition went far beyond mere mechanical prowess. Illegal, high-speed competition out on the streets, one car against another, was the best way to prove one's manhood to the peer group.

Most of the illicit drag racing heats run during the 1950s were arranged at the drive-in restaurant, since that's where the hottest cars and their owners were often parked. Hot rods and cool custom cars were a regular fixture at the drive-in, with the many carhop lanes occupied by gearheads peering intently under their hoods and polishing chrome or tweaking some high-performance goodie. When an interloper with a tough-looking ride pulled in to make a challenge, arrangements were made to meet at a clandestine drag strip usually on the outskirts of town. Like two rabid dogs straining at their leashes, both cars roared out of the drive-in eatery to meet their fate. Only one would claim the victory.

Oscars Drive-In provided the cruisers of the 1950s and the 1960s an appropriate venue to hang out and display their hot rods. Unfortunately, the popular dining spot was eliminated in the name of progress and the cruising fun that was had there remains only as a recollection. *Andy Southard, Jr.*

Hunger, a station wagon full of screaming kids, and a busy mother meant only one thing during the 1950s and 1960s: a trip to the local Steak n' Shake! With window trays stacked to the hilt with Tru-Flavor milkshakes and all sorts of tasty food delights (with chili), it was a time that any hungry child would remember for the rest of his or her life. *CoolStock/photo courtesy Steak n' Shake, Inc., sign Shellee Graham*

The Mercury is one of the standards of the custom car set, as is the Geary location of Mel's Drive-In. This location does a thriving business in the heart of San Francisco and is a favorite place for the locals to dine. It features inside seating that exudes a 1950s-type of nostalgia. *Michael Karl Witzel*

Dallas, Texas, was the origination point of the drive-in eatery and, consequently, had more than its share of curb service restaurants. The Circle Drive-In was a favorite among the teenage crowd of the 1950s, and it became a popular hangout for local students eager to socialize and get a meal. *Dallas Public Library*

On a flat quarter-mile stretch of road, two cars lined up and waited for the signal to hit the gas. If the coast was clear and there was no indication that the cops were cruising nearby, off they went, taking up both lanes of the highway until the faster vehicle pulled ahead and the defeated one broke off. With the winner decided, both racers and the thrill-seeking crowd returned to the drive-in where the winner enjoyed bragging rights for the night. In the movies, it was at this time that the champion met up with the girl of his dreams and they both drove off to meet the dawn of a new day.

Paradoxically, it was the ever-widening popularity of the drive-in restaurant as a cruising destination that contributed to its ultimate downfall and demise. With so many overstimulated teenagers hanging out there around the clock, trouble erupted all too often. On occasion, groups (gangs) from competing schools or car clubs traveled to drive-ins in other towns to stir up trouble. Even among the home team, the friction began to build by the early 1960s: Greasers clad in black leather jackets and ducktail hairdos clashed with socialites in lettermen sweaters. By that time it was more than just Chevy versus Ford; it was the cool against the uncool, black against white, hippie against jock.

With kids in their cars hanging out all night, the drive-in became a no-man's land for the family crowd. In neighborhoods that bordered the popular spots, people complained about the never-ending din of fights, cars burning rubber, and loud rock and roll music. Before too long, the authorities enacted ordinances to restrict the teenagers' movements. Drive-in restaurants began instituting all kinds of rules and regulations, and the entry of cars was closely scrutinized. Now, going to a curb spot to hang out or "loiter" was against the law, as was the repetitious act of cruising up and down the strip. By the 1970s, the freewheeling atmosphere of fun and frolic that was once enjoyed at the drive-in restaurant had diminished considerably. The heyday of cruising the Main for curb service had ended.

By the 1960s, the cruisers visiting the drive-ins were seeing a change in the way carhops looked and dressed. The styles of the era dominated their appearance and it wasn't long before all of the curb girls were decked out in mod hairdos and bell-bottom pants. *Dallas Public Library*

ELLIS ★

CURB SERVICE

PHONE VI. 2-2784

DRIVE-IN
Theatre
and
Restaurant
ROUTE 50
Clarksburg, W. Va.

Close Cover 61 For Safety

THE WILSHIRE

IN

BIG
CHAMP

BIG
CHAMP

X-S

basket
Tacos
dd burger

would never
nal Roberts
was little
etely sur-
exterity
forks
rive-in
are
ay

SENSING the swing of Swank
Wilshire ... for our second
corner (at stand that
There standa
stand
Then
pa
R

... Pico Boulevard

THE DIAMOND

May

CLOSE COVER BEFORE STRIKING MATCH

One Mile West of
POCATELLO

Fine Music Entertainment
Casino

THE RIO CLUB

Pocatello's Night Spot

Pocatello, Idaho

Fred & Kelly's
RESTAURANT

★
GOOD
FOOD
★
ALWAYS
OPEN
★
AIR -
CONDITIONED

Made in U.S.A.
THE DIAMOND MATCH CO. N.Y.C.

Boulevard at

in Ame
great Sa
of Rob
ive-in, th
d in the
— and
Victory
ction in

in the hea
ahuenga,
her Thr
r sup
ine dining room; lunch
nvenient counter or
And for cocktails,
where the clan
sal !

Varsity Waitress Is -

HAPPY TO SERVE YOU

LOCATION

GUEST CHECK NO.

12701

BURBANK ... Victory and Olive Boulevards,

ENCORE OF

e Some Home

Chapter Seven

ARTIFACTS OF THE DRIVE-IN ERA

*T*oday, most of the drive-in restaurants that populated the American roadside during the 1940s, 1950s, 1960s, and even 1970s are gone. On occasion, modern-day motorists may stumble upon decaying remnants of a defunct eatery or a broken sign that once attracted customers with its friendly glow—but these discoveries have quietly become the exception rather than the rule.

With every passing year, the physical evidence of the classic American drive-in restaurant disappears from the roadside scene. With little regard for posterity, the bulk of these former car havens, ice cream shacks, and burger huts are being slated for demolition. To replace them, an endless parade of bigger parking lots, strip malls, and franchised fast-food operations are being planned. All too quickly, the once grand burger huts are fading from memory.

Matchbooks were at one time given away free by the majority of businesses in America. Drive-in restaurants, diners, dry cleaners, and other businesses passed them out to anyone and everyone. Today, they are hoarded by many collectors and join similar articles as reminders of long-defunct operations that once made up the sides of the American streetscape.
Michael Karl Witzel

"Legs," one of Stanley Burke's shapeliest carhop girls, adorned streetside signs, menus, and dinner platters. When Stan's was at the height of its popularity during the 1950s, food was still served with real silverware and plates. For the carhop, carrying two fully loaded trays was formidable. *Michael Karl Witzel*

Fortunately, the foresight of a small minority has allowed for the preservation of a portion of this tasty legacy for future generations. While most of the original architecture typical of the classic styles of decades past has been replaced, a few select artifacts remain that readily conjure up those days of triple-thick milk shakes, double-deck hamburgers, and roller-skating carhops. For curb service aficionados, that's good news.

Still, a few major drive-in touchstones have been saved. Many rare operations that are still in business (such as the Texas Pig Stands) are choosing to restore their big neon signs rather than replace them. Neon that does make it to the junk heap is often snapped up by collectors with the cash to transport it home. But more often than not, the kind of signs that end up in the suburban den are of the simple one- or two-word variety like "Eat" or "Food." The larger, more elaborate marquees end up in museums such as Henry Ford's Greenfield Village or as the centerpiece for a 1950s-retro theme restaurant chain.

For the average drive-in memorabilia collector, a more practical direction is afforded by the various elements that at one time made the drive-in work. Everyday dining utensils such as platters, silverware, drinking glasses, milk shake tumblers, coffee cups, root beer mugs, and window serving trays were at one time an integral part of feeding people in their cars. Best of all, many of these

If one could travel back to an A & W operation of the 1940s, this scene is probably what they would see. These days, heavy glass mugs of the type shown, along with the serving tray that cradled them, have become sought after artifacts to memorialize those drive-in days. *Michael Karl Witzel*

Some collectibles cross over into other categories and as a result are much higher in price and much harder to find for the aficionado of drive-in items. All major soda pop manufacturers produced internally illuminated display units similar to this example, and today they pull down top dollar among those who appreciate vintage ad art. *Michael Karl Witzel*

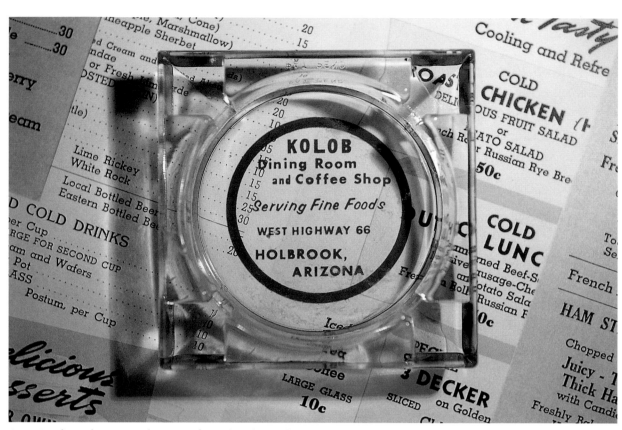

As a simple and easy to obtain artifact, the glass ashtray imprinted with the name and address of a drive-in or other roadside eatery is readily obtained. These holdovers from the days of unlimited smoking in public may be found at flea markets and garage sales nationwide. *Michael Karl Witzel*

practical dining goods were imprinted, engraved, fired, or embossed with logos and trademarks. Since a fair number of car customers sped off with these items to keep as mementos, they are now available to connoisseurs in limited quantities.

Among these "artifacts," the heavy glass serving mugs such as those used by refreshment operations like the A & W Root Beer stands have become immensely desirable. Since the first days of the drive-in restaurants an endless variety of root beer brands were introduced, and it seemed that most all of them had mugs that touted their particular brew. Naturally, the temptation to keep these unique tumblers was overwhelming for

many who liked to drink the sweet, frothy beverage. Many ended up being shoved under the seat and taken home for personal use.

Some car patrons with a bit more nerve decided that the actual food plates, often imprinted with the whimsical depictions of carhops and other such drive-in scenes, would also make neat keepsakes. On one trip, it was quite easy for a plate to be surreptitiously stashed in the glove compartment (40 years ago, these were spacious car cupboards) and on another trip, a coffee cup could be stowed along with the saucer. Over the years, customers who had an inclination toward kleptomania could slowly

Linen postcards are like miniature time capsules. They provide today's viewer (and collector) with a rare opportunity to see what a real drive-in restaurant looked like and the colorful imagery to make the imagination wonder. *Michael Karl Witzel*

acquire an entire set of dishes from their favorite curb service eatery! Is there any wonder why today's fast food restaurants have switched to paper and plastic?

Another important part of the classic drive-in operation was the menu. While a few of them had signboards that listed all of the fare that was available, most of the major operations in California and the Southwest used printed menus to make their entrees known. In the days long before the current limited repertoire of car food outlets

became the norm, elaborate guides showcased the amazing variety of foods that could be served in the front seat of your car. Because each outfit had its own specialty and style of service, these colorful menus became a direct reflection of an eatery's personality.

For today's collector, the drive-in menus that somehow managed to survive and repel the multiple decades of spilled coffee, dripping hot fudge, hamburger grease, and gallons of soft drinks are an excellent way to recall those heady times. After

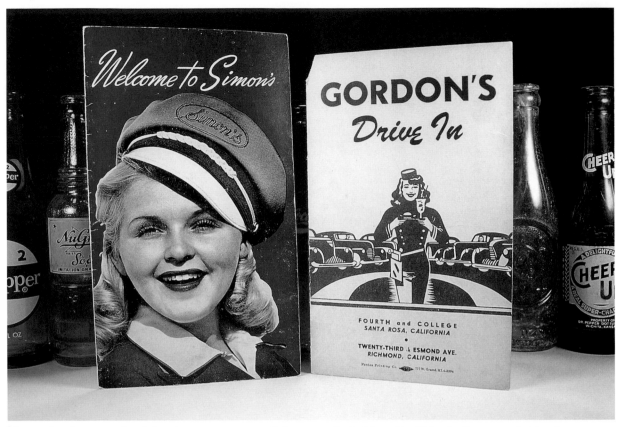

Menus that have survived the decades are one of the most desirable collectibles in the area of drive-in restaurants. Their appeal is varied, providing modern-day scholars a chance to see the changing trends in print advertising and roadside food service. With their splashy colors, funky design, and low prices, they are both a kick to look at and can make a great addition to anyone's collection of carhop memorabilia. *Michael Karl Witzel*

all, the menus that were designed some 40 years ago were bona fide works of art—highly graphic and colorful examples of the day's advertising art. At the same time, they provided a visible showcase for the fashions and attitudes of the carhop waitress. More than any other motif, the combination of a curb gal's smiling face and shapely silhouette was shamelessly exploited on the front cover of nearly every drive-in menu.

While menus were not intended to be carried away, the lion's share of American drive-ins invested capital in printed promotional giveaways of various types. Classified as "ephemera" in the present-day

jargon of collectors, a substantial resource of these fragile handouts have survived the passing decades. In much the same way as the menus do, these advertising artifacts provide the enthusiast with an unobstructed glimpse into the roadside past. Whether these portray "the good old days" or not is up to the individual collector to decide.

In this category of cool stuff culled from the drive-ins, postcards of the penny variety are one of the most hoarded items. At one time in history, they were a major portion of the roadside business ad budget. Across all of the 50 states, it seemed that every wayside snack stand and curb-

"The Burbank" Roberts Brothers drive-in located on Victory and Olive boulevards featured a twisted flash of what appeared to be electricity at the top of its pylon. With circular design, modern equipment, and air-conditioning for inside diners, it was a mecca for motorists in the San Fernando Valley. Today, only menus remain as evidence of the chain. *Author collection*

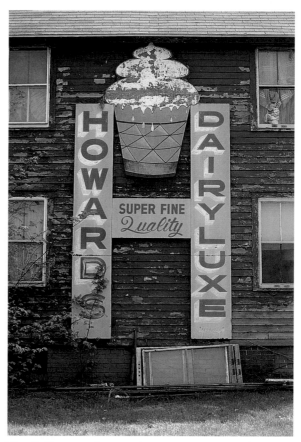

The fluffy-top soft-serve ice cream cone is a frequent motif employed to attract the commuter from his or her route. Everyone loves ice cream. Too bad this sign is all that remains of a former roadside business. *Michael Karl Witzel*

side refreshment stop (large or small) had some sort of imprinted postcard that they handed out. Upon them, satisfied customers touted the specialties that they had consumed and mailed the comments to their friends and family relations. It was a win-win situation for all: Restaurants would get some great publicity and the patron a freebie.

Currently, the so-called "linen" variety of postcards that were produced in great numbers by the Curt Teich Company of Chicago are the most desirable. An enterprising immigrant from Germany, Teich got the notion to make postcards of all types of roadside businesses as far back as 1898. He traveled the country in search of prospects and as a result, myriad roadside operations—drive-ins included—were immortalized in the aspect ratio of 3 1/2x5 inches. Today, the distinctive texture of the crosshatched cardstock that was once used for Teich's tiny billboards is a big part of their vintage appeal, as are the fanciful col-

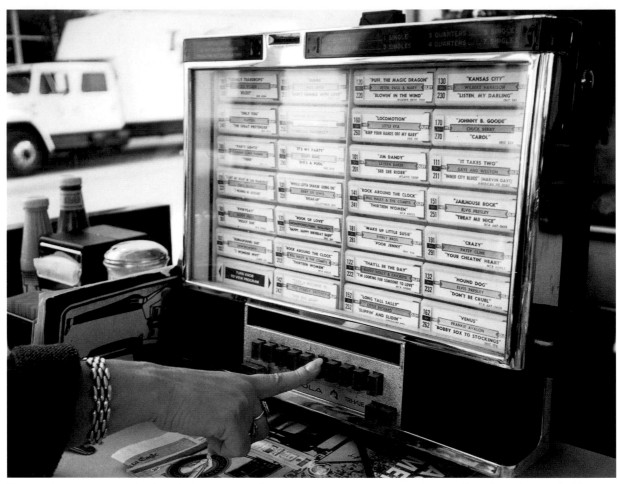

The jukebox was a mechanical device designed to organize and play grooved recording discs for the public. A customer dropped a coin into a slot and selected a song from a list. Push buttons were pressed and a mechanical arm placed the "45" on a turntable platter. A moveable arm housing a "needle" rode the tiny tracks in the disc and transferred minute variations in the vinyl into electrical impulses. An amplifier fed these pulses into a loudspeaker. Before radio was big, musicians relied on jukebox play to gain notoriety. Here, a remote-controlled unit is seen at a California Mel's restaurant. *Michael Karl Witzel*

In 1949, Leo S. Maranz followed the success of Dairy Queen and designed his own automatic ice cream freezer. Unfortunately, he learned that it was too expensive for small businesses to buy unless it came with a franchise to sell ice cream. So, he sold the unit at the manufactured cost to store operators and made his profits on the soft-serve product that was produced by the machines. By June 1953, Tastee-Freez had grown to a national chain with over 600 outlets. *Author Collection/Courtesy Tastee-Freez*

269

oring techniques that his company artists used to retouch scenes in order to make them appear more appealing.

Equally colorful and just as collectible are imprinted matchbooks. Back during the heyday of the drive-ins, some of the major cigarette brands actually promoted the idea that smoking was good for you. Since nearly everyone smoked or aspired to the habit, matchbooks were a really big deal—especially the free ones. Drive-ins didn't miss a beat and picked up on the mandate for after-dinner light-ups. Little match packs splashed with stylized art of every type abounded, filling what-not jars across America until the present day when they have finally reappeared for sale in flea markets and garage sales.

Without a doubt, the demand for drive-in related collectibles and artifacts is growing year by year. Now, even the mainstream marketing gurus are picking up on the craze. Mail-order catalogs with nostalgic sobriquets like "Back to the Fifties" feature a plethora of drive-in type items, all clever reproductions of the genuine articles. Replica window serving trays, complete with a faux milk shake and cheeseburger (made from wax), are some of the most requested items that are sold in the line.

For those with a hankering to relive the drive-in delights of their youth, all of the props required to cruise back into the past are available for purchase, including Coca-Cola button signs, neon clocks, scale models of once famous drive-ins, chrome-plated jukebox radios, and more. In the hearts and minds of motorists and collectors alike, the American drive-in restaurant is back.

Chapter Eight

AMERICAN FAST FOOD FUTURES

When drive-in restaurant owner Troy Smith stopped for lunch at a Louisiana curb service spot back in 1954, he discovered that a clever cable talkback system was being used to gather the customers' food orders. Energized with new enthusiasm, he returned to his hometown of Shawnee, Oklahoma, and immediately hired a local radio repairman to install one of the vacuum tube intercom systems at his own drive-in, a canopy-style eatery called the Top Hat.

Smith's radical order-taking device proved to be the first of its kind in the state. Inspired by the new rate at which orders could be taken and filled, Smith penned the catchy slogan "Service With the Speed of Sound" and made it the creed for his business. This was the beginning of the national Sonic drive-in chain and an entirely new direction

On Golf Road in Schaumburg, Illinois, Portillo's hot dogs employs every trick in the restaurant book to attract patrons beneath its colored bands of neon light. As a food that's easy to make and quite profitable, the hot dog and the many variations of it that may be made is a good choice for an operation that wishes to concentrate on making their specialty the best. *Howard Ande*

273

After Big Boy founder Robert Wian passed on, stewardship of the chunky mascot was assumed by a corporation. As hard as it was for loyal customers to believe, the bean-counters were contemplating his dismissal! After an unfavorable response from the public brought them to their senses, the ousting of the oversized mascot was put to a vote. Should the Big Boy stay or should he go? The answer came back a resounding yes: Americans liked the little butterball and wanted him to stay on as the company greeter and doorman. Nevertheless, some in the radical fringe weren't happy with the decision. The controversy came to a head in 1994 when bandits pilfered a 300-pound, 6-foot-high Big Boy from a Toledo, Ohio, restaurant. Showing little respect for the statue, they dismembered it with a hacksaw and dumped the pieces at Big Boy outlets in the surrounding area. Notes that were attached to the ragged fragments declared: "Big Boy is Dead." This Frisch's model on the old Lincoln Highway remains safe and sound, admired by happy diners. *Michael Karl Witzel*

for the future of curbside service that would one day be exemplified by a total lack of carhops.

With their practicality proven, the rush to install improved electronic ordering networks began in earnest. From 1951 until the end of that decade, a wide range of models were introduced. All the industry publications featured articles on the two-ways, introducing the modern restaurateurs to brands like Aut-O-Hop, Ordaphone, Fon-A-Chef, Serv-us-Fone, Teletray, Dine-A-Mike, TelAutograph, Dine-a-Com, Auto-Dine, and Electro-Hop. Each unit boasted features that included internally lit menus, record changers, dual speech amplifiers, and even the capability to play music. The future of fast food looked so bright that the drive-in owners were reaching for their shades.

While over the next 40 years the Sonic operation remained true to the carhop and speakerbox format, the majority of American fast food outlets chose to go in the direction of service minus the carhops. All too quickly, the energetic curb girl who had rocketed so quickly to icon status during the postwar era became almost extinct. Even the parking lanes where she once strutted her stuff were removed from the equation, replaced by a so-called "drive-thru" window where customers were required to pick up their order and exit to the street. A new-and-improved version of the remote-controlled ordering getup that was popularized by Troy Smith had usurped the responsibilities that were once appointed to a team of individuals.

Today, the modern-day menu board order taker has become the representative monolith for a rushed society that's in too much of a hurry. With a two-way intercom setup at its core and a chaotic patchwork quilt of backlit transparency display areas brimming with saturated, sumptuous-looking photographs of food and beverage choices, these automated service appliances have cleverly replaced all of the features that the drive-in restaurant-goer once held dear. The living, breathing carhop server and the one-on-one interaction that was enjoyed with her (or him) has been reduced to an impersonal two-way conversation via intercom.

The new ordering board has eliminated all need for the neat paper menus that could be held in the hand and studied at one's leisure. Presently, all possible combinations and variations of the basic hamburger and French fry pair-up are listed on the backlit order board, with the resulting conglomerate of information doing more to confuse the arrivee than to inform. Someone unfamiliar with a certain operation's particular food items would be hard-pressed to enjoy an unhurried selection. As cars honk their horns in the line behind, customers must scan and decipher all of the specially grouped meal-deals, combo platters, super-sized entrees, jumbo bags of grub, and other such price-conscious dinner promotions. The uncomplicated days of just pulling up and ordering a plain old cheeseburger are long gone.

At the same time, it's seldom that the consumer comes across one of these menu board gizmos that actually does what it is supposed to do. If the volume on the public address speaker (one that is usually mounted in close proximity to the eardrum and adjusted to a level that can compete with the noise level of a modern airport) isn't too

The Pig Stand sign seen at the San Antonio, Texas, restaurant has recently undergone a facelift. To compete with flashy eateries that line the roadway, neon tubes of searing purple were added to a color scheme that conjures up memories of the 1950s. Here the old sign is seen before the major facelift. *Michael Karl Witzel*

In Webb City, Missouri, the Bradbury Bishop Deli modeled its interior after the vintage soda fountains that were once common. Modern customers enter the nostalgic interior and are immediately transported to the days when milkshakes were made with ice cream and hamburgers were 100 percent beef. *Jim Ross*

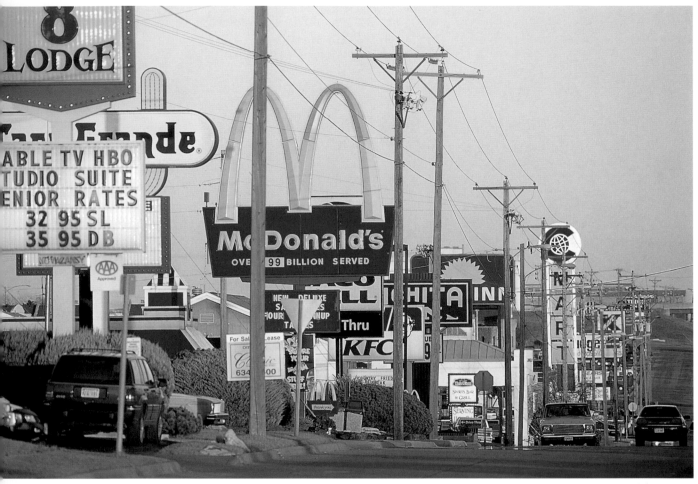

Take a drive into any city today and the view is frighteningly similar: one after another, the very same fast food restaurants are lined up for the car consumer's convenience: Carl's, Wendy's, McDonalds, Burger King, Kentucky Fried Chicken, Whataburger, Taco Bell, Denny's, Spangles, Roy Rogers, Long John Silver's, and many more—they are all there on one strip of well-traveled road, signs shining brightly. *Michael Karl Witzel*

loud, it's way too low and filled with static—making it difficult to hear and understand the order taker cloistered inside the building. If the system happens to be operating at the correct volume level, then the worker inside is untrained in the subtle art of microphone communication.

It should come as no surprise that over the past 30 years, many a comedy sketch has been written and performed about this particular prob-

lem. It seems that no matter what amazing advancements in electronic intercommunication technology come down the pike, there's no relief in sight. During the 1970s the motoring fast food eaters of America nodded in affirmation and smiled quietly when the Jack-in-the-Box hamburger organization blew up their own speaker box clown in a series of hilarious television commercials. For a brief moment in the history of road-

Amid a panoply of competing restaurants and hamburger joints, it's difficult for even the most modern "theme restaurant" to withstand the pressure from the competition. Automotive-oriented restaurants like Hudson's appear—and then disappear—in the southern California region faster than you can dip two scoops and mix a double milkshake. *Kent Bash*

side food, one of the major players acknowledged the public's frustration and relieved some of the tension.

But a lot more has changed since the crazy days of the classic drive-in restaurant than just the intercom setup used to make faster orders. In the area of internal ordering protocols, the once whimsical banter that was exchanged between the order taker and the grill cook has been permanently eliminated. Where at one time a carhop might have called out loud to place her order for an "airdale" and a "stretch," special codes are now

279

Specialized hamburger outlets such as Rally's have given the big burger corporations a run for their money. Using nostalgic touches like glass brick, circular porthole windows, and neon lights, they appeal to the baby-boomer crowd that's interested in food quality and customer service. *Howard Ande*

being entered into a computer keyboard to signify the hot dog and Coke combination. At the twentieth-century hamburger bars of America, there's no room for folksy slang terms or friendly chatter.

Nowadays, the qualities of speed, efficiency, and customer turnover have been driven to the forefront. Instantaneously, the customer's selection is transmitted by bits and bytes along a maze of wiring to be displayed in contrasting type on a series of green cathode ray tubes that are mounted throughout the prep area. In this new Orwellian environment, duplicate television screens hang above the grill and checkout window, allowing all personnel to visually confirm at any

Detroit's Woodward Avenue is famous for the street machines that used to drive up the strip back in the 1950s and 1960s. Today, the essence of those times may be seen in restaurants along the entire length of this once hectic hot rod venue. The America Restaurant in Royal Oak recalls those drive-in cruising days with an unselfish use of classic materials. *Howard Ande*

given moment what "order is up" and where it is going. Despite these overly complex systems, human error is still a factor and mistakes in one's order are still made.

Still, it's not always the fault of these unsung fast food workers if an order is prepared incorrectly. The roadside playing field has changed dramatically since Richard and Maurice McDonald slapped

their first hamburger patty on the grill. These days, most of the roadside eateries are expanding their menus to gigantic proportions. Where at one time it was perfectly acceptable to sell only the standard food items, today's eateries are attempting to fulfill all of the consumers' desires. As a result, many unrelated entrees—including chef salads, pizza pies, dessert cakes, apple fritters, pita pocket

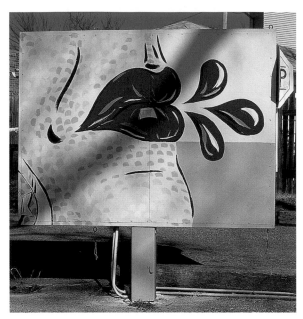

While most of the ordering boards of present-day fast food assume similar shapes, one may occasionally find a whimsical creation that's ready to take your food order. This big-lipped intercom board greets cars in Wichita, Kansas. *Michael Karl Witzel*

While deceptively simple on the exterior, the complexity of the sno-cone lies in its execution and creation. Yet, the elementary process of creating one is quite easy if you possess the knack for it. Dale's Sno-Cone stand in River Oaks, Texas, still follows the same classic method it has for decades. Owner Mamie Dale makes sure of it! Practicing her skillful methods every summer, Mamie established the criteria other stands are judged by and has proven that in the rare instance, the individually owned and operated stand can remain a viable force. *Michael Karl Witzel*

sandwiches, hoagies, chocolate chip cookies, ice cream cakes, sticky buns, egg rolls, and more—are being offered for sale to the modern consumer.

Instead of filling a niche market like the early pioneers of the fast food industry once did, roadside food chains are slowly reverting back to the drive-in days of the 1920s and 1930s when everything under the sun was served for general consumption. While on the surface this movement toward total inclusiveness might appear to be a boon for the traveling diner, the matter is up for debate. After all, certain entrees are specialties in themselves and aren't always conducive to the assembly-line processes that are employed by the roadside restaurant industry. Further expansion of the fast food menu board might water down the reputation attained from established food items.

However, there are a few select chain operations that are choosing to stick with the tried-and-true formula of selling just the staple items of favorite American road food. Rather than adding on exotic new meals, they concentrate on perfecting the mainline menu items and work to make them the best that they can be in terms of quality and taste. Efficient drive-in drive-through stands with names like Checkers, Burger Street, Rally's, and In–N–Out Burger are appearing on vacant parking lot spaces across the country, proving to the rest of the fast food industry that the basic hamburger and soft drink menu is more than enough to remain competitive on the roadside playing field.